CW01220692

RAYMOND CHANDLER

RAYMOND CHANDLER

ANTHONY FOWLES

GE

Greenwich Exchange
London

Greenwich Exchange, London

First published in Great Britain in 2014
All rights reserved

Raymond Chandler © Anthony Fowles 2014

This book is sold subject to the conditions that it shall not, by way of trade or otherwise, be lent, resold, hired out or otherwise circulated without the publisher's prior consent in any form of binding or cover other than that in which it is published and without a similiar condition including this condition being imposed on the subsequent purchaser.

Printed and bound by imprintdigital.net
Cover design by December Publications
Tel: 028 90 286559

Greenwich Exchange Website: www.greenex.co.uk

Cataloguing in Publication Data is available from the British Library

Cover art: Mary Evans Picture Library

ISBN: 978-1-906075-87-3

for Orla

'He was therefore obliged to seek some other means of support; and having no profession, became by necessity an author.'
— Samuel Johnson: *The Life of Richard Savage.*

CONTENTS

    Chronology *13*

1   The Short Stories *25*

2   The Big Sleep *48*

3   Philip Marlowe *68*

4   Farewell, My Lovely *77*

5   The High Window *94*

6   The Lady in the Lake *108*

7   Chandler in Hollywood *125*

8   The Long Goodbye *142*

9   Playback *162*

10   Conclusion *172*

    Bibliography *195*

    Index *199*

Chronology

1888   Chandler (christened Raymond Thornton) born on July 23 in Chicago a year after the marriage of his American father to an Irish woman, Florence Thornton, who had come to America to holiday with a married sister. Both the parents are of Quaker stock.

1895   Maurice Chandler proves to be a dedicated alcoholic and fecklessly deserts wife and son. Florence secures a divorce. Briefly staying with her American in-laws in Nebraska, she is driven to return to her native Waterford so as to guarantee a roof over her head. Her mother, feeling that Florence has disgraced the family by marrying beneath her is less than pleased.

1895   Florence moves to Norwood in South London where her brother Ernest grudgingly agrees to shelter her and his nephew. A prosperous solicitor working both sides of the Irish Channel, Ernest Thornton is aloof but provides financial security.

1900   Thornton arranges for Raymond to attend Dulwich College as a day boy. It is a crucial opportunity for him to better himself. Under the benign Headmastership of the classicist A.H. Gilkes, Dulwich offers an enlightening curriculum and Chandler consistently performs well right across the academic board. His fragmented background, however – three countries, one parent, uncertain family income – make him difficult to pigeon-hole and incipiently independent.

1905 Chandler leaves Dulwich. His uncle has not thought a University education is a viable (financial) option but is willing to stake his nephew to a 'gap year' in Europe which will enable him to perform well in the Language section of the Civil Service Exams. The strategy is that Raymond will aim for a respectable career in the Civil Service. Six months in first Paris and then South Germany add fluency to his schoolboy French and German.

1907-11 At eighteen Chandler passes third out of 600 candidates in the Civil Service Exam. He is first in the Classics paper. He accepts a junior position in the Admiralty thinking that a routine job will allow him time to develop as a writer but after six months of suffering 'suburban nobodies' resigns – thus affronting his uncle and horrifying his mother.

He proceeds to spend four years 'holing out' on the margins of Bloomsbury eventually moving to cheap lodgings in Russell Square. During this period he writes a good deal of quite execrable sub-Dowson, sub-Binyon 'Georgian' verse some of which earns publication in little magazines. He also contributes occasional, quite discerning, book reviews to the

Westminster Gazette. To make ends meet he is obliged to return to Dulwich College as, in effect, a supply teacher.

1912   Ends not adequately meeting, Chandler opts to return to America. He borrows the fare from his uncle and, as befits a young man, goes West. A series of *ad hoc* jobs take him to San Francisco where, realizing he needs a solid qualification, he enrols in a night school and in six weeks covers a three-year accountancy course. So equipped he obtains a position as book-keeper in a Los Angeles dairy products organization. It is as a book-keeper that he spends his first three years in the city that he will, in a fashion, immortalize.

1917   Very conscious of the wholesale sacrifice being made by England's doomed public school youth Chandler enlists in the Canadian Army, joining the Gordon Highlanders in Vancouver. By November he is in England.

1918   Chandler is shipped to France in early spring. In June he is in the trenches. A German bombardment hits his battalion's position and he is possibly the sole survivor. Seriously concussed, he is shipped back to England where after convalescence he is transferred into the Royal Air Corps. In four months he learns to fly and, significantly, how to drink. At the age of twenty-six he has developed a taste for alcohol. The Armistice precludes his return to active service as a pilot.

1919 Back in America via Vancouver, and a civilian again, Chandler spends a year in Seattle and San Francisco doing short-term stints of casual work. He is intermittently writing both poetry and prose but in no way that catches a commercial eye.

1920 Returned to Los Angeles Chandler is indebted to wealthy acquaintances who secure him a job with a newly-founded oil company, the Dabney Oil Syndicate. Oil is just beginning to gush in Southern California and the company goes from strength to strength. Chandler acting as a *de facto* actuary-cum-office manager rises along with it. His intelligence enabling him to catch a superior embezzling, he ends by taking over the man's position. For the first time in his life he is well off. He becomes keenly attracted to a woman he meets socially – a Cissy Pascal. She is ten years his senior and trails an interesting past. When working in New York as a model she did not baulk at posing nude. There are rumours of her having found opium congenial. Divorced once, she is currently married to a close friend of Chandler's benefactors. They are understanding and 'adult' about the new development but during Chandler's war time absence the Pascals had housed and looked after his mother whom he had supportively brought to America. Florence Chandler, abandoned by her own husband, cannot condone Cissy deserting hers. She bitterly opposes the prospect of Chandler making Mrs Pascal a wife for the third time.

1924 Florence dies of cancer in late January. In early February Chandler and Cissy marry. It is universally recognised that she is ethereally beautiful and nobody can believe that she is ten years his senior. Nor is she. Eventually Chandler will learn that he has been lied to and that his wife is almost twenty years the older.

1932 Chandler is fired from his old company job – with reason. Over the past five years or more he has become a seriously heavy drinker sometimes going on benders that have led to him blacking out. He has arrived at work visibly the worse for drink – or not arrived at all. Worse, he has indulged in an affair with a work colleague whose office performance has become matchingly unacceptable. Shocked into sobriety by this return to unemployment Chandler considers options. His literary fancy has been taken by the worth he has detected in the Dashiell Hammett-style short stories featured in such pulp fiction magazines as *Black Mask*. As when crash-coursing accountancy, Chandler enrols in a creative writing evening class. The better to understand their mechanics he strips down published stories to bald plot analyses and then rewrites them in his own style. He begins to write original stories.

1933 Chandler sells his first short story 'Blackmailers Don't Shoot' to *Black Mask*. At the age of forty-four and just when Dashiell Hammett's alcoholism is ending his own career, Chandler is in danger of becoming a professional author. In the course of the next six years Chandler sees a further twenty of his stories published. Given the 'cent a word' going rate and his insistence on reworking and repolishing, this still leaves him under financial siege but his name is now the one pulp fiction devotees look for. Throughout this period Chandler remains rigidly teetotal and scrupulously monitors his wife's increasing ill-health.

1938 A New York agent shows Chandler's short-story work to the major publisher Alfred Knopf who is sufficiently impressed to commission a novel-length thriller.

1939 Chandler now fifty-one years old, *The Big Sleep* is published by Knopf in America and in England by Hamish Hamilton. Adequately promoted but little reviewed it achieves modestly acceptable sales.

1940 *Farewell, My Lovely* published.

1942 *The High Window* published.

1943 *The Lady in the Lake* published. All Chandler's novels have achieved sales little more than adequate but word-of-mouth recommendations are beginning to win him a 'cult' following. Further, impressed by *The High Window*, a Paramount producer invites Chandler to work with Billy Wilder on adapting *Double Indemnity* for the screen. Hollywood considers the project a poisoned chalice as Cain's novel surely contains too much sex and violence to gain approval from the prudishly servile Production Code authority. Chandler and Wilder are never soulmates but they have sufficient mutual respect to allow their respective talents to mesh. Subtly allusive, the script passes muster and the film becomes an instant, universal and enduring success. Chandler's fortunes have been transformed: with one bound Hollywood rates have made him fiscally free.

1944   *Farewell, My Lovely* – filmed for a second time by RKO who own the rights. Chandler, at Paramount, is not involved.

1945   Chandler writes an original screenplay *The Blue Dahlia*. Since its star, Alan Ladd, is imminently due to be drafted, he is obliged to do this against the clock. His drinking escalates as he resorts to alcohol to ease the pressure.

1945   *The Big Sleep*, directed by Howard Hawks, is bought and released by Warner Brothers. Contracted to Paramount, Chandler is excluded from formal involvement. In late summer Chandler breaks new ground. He buys a house. It is mint new and on the idyllic Southern Californian coast at La Jolla just north of San Diego. Thus ends three decades of living in literally several dozen short-term rented addresses across and around greater Los Angeles. Chandler and Cissy will live here uninterruptedly and in semi-reclusion for the next eight and a half years as she becomes increasingly a victim of fibrosis of the lungs. Chandler acts as her housekeeper, cook, nurse and chauffeur throughout this period.

1946   Chandler is commissioned by Universal Studios to write an original screenplay. In La Jolla his drinking is under reasonable control and he duly completes a final draft entitled *Playback*. Universal, however, is facing bankruptcy and decides it must write off an 'expensive' location-based project as a tax loss.

1949   *The Little Sister* published. Chandler had begun this some three years earlier while still at Paramount. He has found completing it an uphill task involving much re-writing and fluctuating misgivings.

1950   Alfred Hitchcock, through Warner Brothers, asks Chandler to adapt Patricia Highsmith's *Strangers on a Train* for the screen. Chandler agrees but it is a union made in Hollywood not heaven. Hitchcock's concern is with (visual) form; Chandler's is with content. More profoundly their distinctive egos are at odds. The partnership is broken off within weeks.

1952   Chandler takes the ailing Cissy on a long anticipated visit to London – his first visit in forty years. She is not up to the rigours of travelling and the treat becomes a near disaster.

1953   *The Long Goodbye* published in England in November and in America two months later. Chandler has no financial worries but between his drinking and his ministering to Cissy his own health is indifferent and his energy levels low. Laboriously writing and rewriting over a period of some three years Chandler indicates that this is to be a 'big' book – and that it will mark Philip Marlowe's last appearance.

1954   At the very end of the year Cissy dies. Chandler is distraught.

1955   In February, ten weeks after his wife's death Chandler is the centre of a comic-grim episode. After he calls the La Jolla police stating that he intends to kill himself they discover him in his shower – still alive. A gun has been fired but either this is a 'conventional' cry for help incident or Chandler, given to blackouts when drunk, has acted inadvertently. Conceivably it is a genuine attempt on his own life that has misfired. Friends install Chandler in a sanatorium. Within a week he has convinced all and sundry of his being a balanced personality again. Within two more weeks he has sold the La Jolla house. In April

Chandler travels to London. Here his behaviour becomes embarrassingly off-kilter. He drinks like a fish and develops the habit of asking virtually every woman who crosses his path to marry him. A 'team' of cultured friends do all they can to mitigate these descents into humiliating fantasy proposals. An attempt to avoid paying U.K. taxes returns him to the US but finding America now 'bores' him he returns to England in December.

1956   For four months Chandler is a soft-headed loose cannon on the British literary-publishing scene. By June, somewhat steadier, he returns to America and rents an apartment in La Jolla. Despite his previous announcement he picks up his *Playback* screenplay and begins to re-work it as a novel with Marlowe as the investigating protagonist.

1957   Although drinking more heavily than he has allowed himself to do so during the writing of any other work, Chandler finishes *Playback* just before Christmas.

1958   *Playback* published. It is generously but 'kindly' received. Chandler spends most of the year oscillating between La Jolla and London – and between various putative brides-to-be. He is in and out of clinics both sides of the Atlantic.

1959   March, very much the worse for drink, he dies in

the same La Jolla hospital as Cissy. Among his papers is found the first draft opening of what might have become another Marlowe story, 'Poodle Springs'. In time this will be continued by another writer. This venture will provide agreeable revenues for publishers and agents but will do Chandler's posthumous reputation considerable disservice.

The Short Stories

IN 1913, IN HIS MID-TWENTIES, AND in San Francisco, Raymond Chandler must have sensed Time was running out on him. Since his return to America a year earlier he had found work in no more than a series of short-order service industry jobs. Clearly an English public school education, a brief period as a Junior English Civil Servant and a few years failing to impact upon the Bloomsbury literary scene cut no ice at all out here on the West Coast. If he was ever to open the door upon a more rewarding, long-term career he must obtain a more tangible qualification.

Enrolling in an accountancy evening class Chandler did exactly that. He combined the discipline he had acquired at Dulwich College with his native wits to such good effect that he completed the three-year course in just six weeks. By 1914 he was holding down a position in the accounts department of a dairy products company in – significantly – Los Angeles. In due course – a course interrupted by front-line service in the World War One trenches

– he had translated himself from milk to oil. He speedily became *de facto* actuary of a burgeoning Southern Californian oil company. It was a shrewd translation. Oil was just about the one exception to the plummeting economic trends which on a personal level, married now, Chandler had bucked. Born in Chicago rather than St Louis he had climbed a goodly way up the ladder of comfortable success. A dozen years later all was changed utterly. In 1932 Chandler found himself slithering down one of Life's spectacularly unpleasant snakes. He had got himself fired.

He had only himself to blame. The taste for consuming binge-drinking quantities of booze that his War years had fostered had finally caught up with him. He had become capable of drinking himself into a blacked-out stupor over several days of absenteeism. The Dabney Oil Syndicate might just possibly have overlooked such gross misconduct given the overall excellence of his work but since he latterly had induced the colleague with whom he was conducting a flagrantly obvious extra-marital affair to mimic his alcohol and 'sick leave' pattern it had, finally, no option. Chandler was out on his forty-four-year-old ear. Some money in the Savings and Loan apart, he was back where he had been two decades earlier. The Depression was at its lowest slump. Time, once more, to buckle down.

Contrite – his affection for his wife was an abiding factor in his life – Chandler steeled himself to do just that. But ... what?

In his callow, imitative Bloomsbury youth Chandler had played at being a poet, a journalist, a reviewer – some kind of writer. The itch had never quite deserted him. One day, perhaps ... And now, needs musting, this might have to be the day. Something had latterly caught his eye. A relatively new phenomenon was out there on the news stands – pulp magazines, such as *Black Mask, Dime Detective Monthly, Action Detective*. Pungent, low-life crime stories were their stock in trade written as luridly as the covers were garish and, of course, in no way could they be classed as literature. Booth Tarkington didn't write for them; or Louis Bromfield or Joseph Hergesheimer. But Dashiell Hammett did. He had set out a style and standard that had caught Chandler's attention. Hammett's work, he strongly suspected, couldn't be written off quite that readily. Eighteen years later he was to write to his London publisher:

> A Classical education helps you from being fooled by pretentiousness, which is what most current fiction is too full of. In this country the mystery writer is looked down on as a sub-literary merely because he is a mystery writer, rather than for instance a writer of social significance twaddle. To a classicist – even a very rusty one – such an attitude is merely a parvenu insecurity.

The word 'classicist' as attached to Chandler must be central to any attempt to assess his work. Rusty he may have become (although we may confidently believe him to have retained as much Latin and Greek as we are led to believe Shakespeare possessed) but Dulwich College would have left him permanently aware of this hugely pregnant critical perception: whenever Homer takes the trouble to describe a sword it is because somebody is about to use it. Meanwhile, however, forget Homer. A going rate of a cent a word would be better than standing in line for a soup kitchen hand-out.

As in his self-imposed crash accountancy course Chandler applied himself with commendably pragmatic concentration. One dime magazine writer he admired was Erle Stanley Gardner. Taking a Gardner story he stripped it down as, the better to see how it functioned, a motor mechanic might take apart an engine. In 1939, writing now as equal to equal, Chandler acknowledged his debt in a letter.

> I made an extremely detailed synopsis of your story and from that rewrote it and then compared what I had with yours, and then went back and rewrote it some more, and so on. In the end I was a bit sore because I couldn't try to sell it.

Nevertheless the more important objective had been achieved. The moment came when, feeling he had completed his apprenticeship, the forty-four year old sat down to write his first original crime story.

'Blackmailers Don't Shoot' is some 18,000 words in length. It took him five months to write – a month for each of the versions he completed before feeling able to submit it to *Black Mask*. This insistence upon taking repeated pains was to be a key characteristic of Chandler's working practice. But in this initial step into professional authorship he was not entirely taking his time so as to traffic in subtle nuance. Throwing caution to the winds he erred on the side of violence – violence ricocheted about by characters reached down from the ready-made shelf. They are all as stock as two-dimensional. Chandler recycles the handsome, steely-eyed and -minded private eye; the coarsely corrupt and run-to-fat cop; the suavely elegant but fatally flawed and disillusioned night-spot owner; the homicidally psychopathic hitman, the ineffably beautiful femme fatale. These types are choreographed in an acceleratingly vehement dance of dime-magazine death as the gunplay starts to confirm that the story's title is nothing but sardonic. All plot is out the window. The incriminating letters may or may not be forged. The shady lawyer may be pulling the blackmail strings or it may be the night-spot racketeer. Or is it all a misfiring publicity stunt? Who cares? As we read rapidly on we are not concerned to find out. As, against all commonsense, life-preserving logic, character after character puts himself on the line the more totally to be gunned down, the foreground is everything. We've no inclination on this first reading to step back and analyse the utter implausibility, the completely irrational motivations which have successively propelled the puppets into Chandler's line of fire. We accept, in fact, that he is offering us here a holiday from logic and morality and, as we do with many a Hammett story, we gleefully accept the second-hand adrenalin rush which the double crossing, wham-bam gun play triggers.

Chandler himself acknowledged as much when in an authorized re-issue of some of his pulp stories he addressed this very topic.

> Undoubtedly the stories ... had a fantastic element. Such things happened but not so rapidly, nor to so close-knit a group of people, nor within so narrow a frame of logic. This was inevitable because the demand was for constant action; if you stopped to think you were lost. When in doubt have a man come through a door with a gun in his hand. This could get to be pretty silly, but somehow it didn't seem to matter.

Well, not immediately, not always. In the instance of

'Blackmailers Don't Shoot' there is an eventual down-side. It lacks, by and large, the finesse in plot construction, the ironic and elegant reversal of fortune, the sociological sub-text that might cause it to resonate in the mind and so lure us back to savour its artfulness a second time. A first shot at the pulp market, when all is said and done, it may be looked upon as Chandler's anticipation of a spaghetti Western.

Yet, on consideration, this may be too damning a verdict. If we shift our focus from plot mechanics to the surface structure of the story, its prose, its words on the page, we may well decide it contains lasting qualities. Even on our first helter-skelter reading certain individual words – *morosely, languid, opaque, wizened, sibilant* – may well have registered above the level of our subconscious intake. In the night a man's overcoat is *indistinct*. A newly-minted corpse, the same man, now smells '*violently* of whisky.' This is not the vocabulary or quite the phraseology that Hammett with his resolutely dead-pan and largely adverb-free prose employs. Even when addressing the pulp market the first time around Chandler is willing to trust himself and his reader to function at a certain level of literacy. These are literary words. Here is an author concerned to polish his prose. And perhaps offer us more.

Early on in 'Blackmailers Don't Shoot' Chandler describes his femme fatale as she comes under pressure:

> Her eyes looked like the prelude to a scream.

This is a well-turned sentence. It gives off an arresting vibration. It is, on examination, a perfect iambic pentameter. It could almost be taken from a Jacobean drama. Rhonda Farr's eyes look like the prelude to a scream because she has realized that now is the winter of her discontent. Now, to an English reader's ear at least, there is something distinctly potent about the rhythm of the pentameter. Chandler, as a pupil at Dulwich College would have been literally well versed in Shakespeare (and, indeed, in time would allude to *Richard III* in one of his Marlowe novels). I am not, of course, stating that he ever at any time consciously conceived that a work entitled 'Blackmailers Don't Shoot' should come before the world in so many thousand lines of blank verse: but I do suggest that somewhere just below his immediately calculating writer's mind there existed a potent reservoir of nourished literary awareness. I cite in support another giant. At the height of his fame and powers Charles Dickens howled in complaint to John Forster his friend, quasi-agent and eventual biographer, that when writing under the pressures exerted by serial deadlines he found it next to impossible to avoid writing sentence after sentence with the same Shakespearean pentameter cadence to their conclusions. Thus he inserted rhythmical monotony. Perhaps in some celestial Mermaid Tavern Dickens, Shakespeare and Chandler (and William Faulkner!) have sat comparing notes. If so, Chandler, though suitably modest, no doubt, would not have been out of place. I paint this amiable picture to illustrate that one of the lasting virtues of even so early a Chandler story as 'Blackmailers Don't Shoot' is that it foreshadows, already exhibits, his ability to instil momentum and a constantly renewing freshness into his narrative through his control of the cadence and rhythm of his prose. It is a quality only to be truly appreciated over a sustained reading – let me take it then as read – but he is a writer who at his best makes words and syllables give us a sense of inevitable exactitude as they fall into place on the beat.

There is another aspect to Rhonda Farr's eyes looking like the prelude to a scream. What makes this expression arresting is its degree, essentially subliminal, of compression. Of poetic compression. There is a telescoping here of the visual and the aural. Prosaically spelt out the sentence would read something along the insipid lines of: the expression in her eyes changed to one of alarm so that it seemed as if she were on the point of screaming out loud. But, in a way that would have delighted Miss Groby, Chandler makes 'the eyes' an example of 'the container for the thing contained' and dramatically half implies that it will be from the eyes and not the mouth that the scream will issue. We might just be put in mind of Mark Antony standing over the corpse of Caesar and likening its freshly-opened stab wounds to 'dumb mouths' that are begging him to speak on Caesar's behalf. Or again, while it is perhaps unlikely that at Dulwich College circa 1904 Chandler was much encouraged to read John Donne, we might detect a fleck of Metaphysical poetic technique in the juxtapositioning of eyes and screaming. This is probably to overstate; and it risks belabouring the superfluous to spell all this out at length but I think the emphasis is justified. It serves to flag up that although he was to write in an allegedly minor genre throughout his career Chandler claimed membership of a major literary tradition and that he was able to draw upon the inheritance that tradition had given him to nourish his own work. Despite his having gone to school on Erle Stanley Gardner and despite the template example set a decade earlier by Hammett's determinedly undeviating, flat paratactic style, Chandler even at the outset of his career had the courage occasionally to introduce into his prose that variation – a subtle flavour of elegance – which his 'literary' education had given him as a resource. He was to continue doing so throughout all the work that was to follow. It is a truth requiring to be universally acknowledged that a major element in reading Chandler is the immediate local pleasure we derive from the ordering of words on the page. If we leap forward now seven years to his first novel-length Marlowe story, we find, I believe, an almost specific example of his ability to redeploy to advantage his Dulwich classroom past. *The Big Sleep* has as fine a valedictory conclusion as any twentieth-century novel – *All Quiet on the Western Front* included. It begins:

> What did it matter where you lay once you were dead? In a dirty sump or in a marble tower on top of a high hill? You were dead, you were sleeping the big sleep, you were not bothered by things like that. Oil and water were the same as wind and air to you. You just slept the big sleep, not caring about the nastiness of how you died or where you fell.

With that 'marble tower', I suggest, we receive a subliminal flashback of Chandler R. in A.H. Gilkes' Classics set. The tower is not in Forest Lawn. It is the tower the building of which Achilles and Sarpedon and other heroes from *The Iliad* wanted above all else – not to mark their passing but that the subsequent generations of men might admire how they had lived their lives. High-falutin' and then some! But the touch of (literary) class serves to emphasise both the sordidness of Rusty Regan's ending and the source of the Sternwood fortune. And it sets Marlowe up for his own return to earth.

On the way downtown I stopped at a bar and had a couple of double Scotches. They didn't do me any good. All they did was made me think of Silver Wig, and I never saw her again.

Sunt lacrimae rerum indeed!

In the pursuit of variation Chandler had a far more immediate means at his disposal than occasional and oblique literary references and constructions. A huge proportion of his stories and novels is made up of dialogue – of tough, confrontational, insulting, wise-cracking, street-talk dialogue. Having lived successively in America, Ireland and England by the time he was eight he must have learnt to adjust to local speech rhythms, vocabularies and jargon at his mother's and all her relatives' knees. Dulwich gave him insight into the structure of language. And while I think we should take with a large pinch of salt his claim – in a letter as late as 1957 to a Californian High School teacher fan – that after six months in Germany he could pass as native born, he was clearly a very able linguist. Later, forever switching social strata and milieux, moving from one Los Angeles neighbourhood to another, he must have been constantly attuned to the differences in demotic that the failure of the American melting pot ever to coalesce entirely can throw up just one block on from the next. He came hugely to admire the pungent directness of everyday American expression – that sharpness which means that while an Englishman may only mend a puncture, an American can fix a flat. In time he was acclaimed for his use of slang and regarded as something of an expert. Or so regarded himself. In another letter – to Hamish Hamilton in 1950 – he was not backward in coming forward to take Eric Partridge, the celebrated authority on English slang, to task in respect of a series of 'inaccurate' glosses. And certainly 'Blackmailers Don't Shoot' shows us Chandler slanging away like there would be no tomorrow.

Wiper, punk, gumshoe, creep. Stopped lead, cheap chiseller, ditch the hot one and drive this heap. The slang words and expressions come hot and heavy, punctuating the more leisurely expositional prose and the more civilized conversations. In fact, since so much slang idiom is ephemeral and we are (currently) eight decades on from the original writing, it is hard at times for us to judge whether or not Chandler went over the top in a too flashy attempt to impress us with his mastery of low-life idiom. When he writes

> She hired me to put Landrey on the spot. I played along with him until I got him under the gun of a wiper that was pretending to make a pass at me. The wiper let him have it, and I shot the wiper with Landrey's gun to make it look good.

it could reasonably be argued that Chandler is dangerously close to anticipating S.J. Perelman's pitch-perfect parody *Farewell, My Lovely Appetiser*. Not that it matters. For us today the slang works in context and has period charm. For the guy in 1932 who forked across his dime it was just the fix his think-tank was crying out for. And certainly Chandler paid his researcher's dues. Looking back in some tranquility in 1949, he wrote to a Canadian correspondent Alex Barris:

> I had to learn American just like a foreign language. To learn it I had to study and analyse it. As a result, when I

use slang, colloquialisms, snide talk or any kind of offbeat language I do it deliberately ... I've found that there are only two kinds that are any good: slang that has established itself in the language and slang that you make up for yourself.

He sure says a mouthful there.

In 'Blackmailers Don't Shoot' the plot is token, the foreground action and momentum everything. At times seeking to find – give vent to, rather – his own voice he overcooks his ingredients and succumbs to the temptation of 'fine' (and bumptious) writing. He is over-indulgent when he had his femme fatale come out with this:

> 'I loathe these dives,' she said thinly. 'They look as if they only existed after dark like ghouls. The people are dissipated without grace, sinful without irony.'

Too much, if it is meant straight. It makes us wonder if he sat next to Thesiger or Crawley one way-back-when night in Soho. And, if it is intended to indicate the speaker's phoniness, it is implausibly out of character. A Hollywood actress on the skids doesn't possess such power of pretentious observation.

But such is already the exception. Already in 'Blackmailers Don't Shoot' Chandler is hitting on as functional a length as: 'Her voice was small and tired but her chin stuck out hard and brave'. Indeed, in the main, 'Blackmailers Don't Shoot' already contains in embryo all the virtues of Chandler's later books – the smooth texture of the controlled and varied prose; the sharp tang of streetwise exchange when push comes to confrontation; the wit whereby nearly everyone, Chandler included, gets to crack wise when the moment occurs. And, oh yes –

> Mardonne flipped his brown hands up and down on the chair like a purchasing agent getting restless under a sales talk.

– already there are forerunners of the sardonically apt and witty similes that were to become the defining hallmark of the Chandler/Marlowe DNA.

Chandler had prised open an entry into the pulp fiction market and over the next seven or so years around twenty further short crime stories followed. It was a long way from the prolific output of Gardner: but long enough to make it tedious now to pick through each story in turn. One, however, published as late as 1939, merits a passing mention in dispatches because it is unique in the Chandler canon – a genuine Chandler sport.

'Pearls are a Nuisance' is a crime story surely enough involving jewel theft and double-cum-triple crossing. But its protagonist is no jaded private eye down to his last five spot whom we meet cooling his heels on the edge of his desk as he watches a fly circle in the stale air of a client-free office. Measured against Marlowe's bank book Walter Gage is as rich as Croesus – as befits not a gum-shoe but an East Coast, Ivy League gentlemen of independent means. He does not while away his leisure hours scanning well-turned ankles in downtown bars. He has an opposite number fiancée – sic – who is as jolly lacrosse-sticks wholesome as her honour is bright and, verily, in matters of the bedroom Walter verges on the virginal. He is, however, a hunk, or, rather, a *homo athleticus* clearly capable of winning his half blue as a Rhodes

Scholar heavyweight. Walter, in truth, comes as near to being an English gentleman as Chandler could have drawn him without locating him on the further side of the Atlantic. Where this upper-class polish most manifests itself is in Walter's diction; the way in which he talks and, since 'Pearls are a Nuisance' is written in the first person, narrates. His speech patterns are those of an English QC. Chandler is playing for laughs here and to point the jest he has circumstances team Walter up – after a fashion – with his American dead opposite. Henry Eichelberger packs just as meaty a heavyweight punch, true, but Henry is strictly from the wrong side of the tracks – from cow college and a sojourn or two in the State Pen. It's a happy formula. Chandler is able to work both sides of his personal trans-Atlantic verbal spectrum.

> 'Say, you're drunk,' Henry said with admiration in his small green eyes.
> 'I am not yet drunk, Henry, although I do in fact feel the effect of that whisky and very pleasantly. You must not mind my way of talking which is a personal matter, like your own clipped and concise method of speech. But before we depart there is one rather insignificant detail I wish to discuss with you. I am empowered to arrange the return of Mrs Penruddock's pearls. I understand there is some possibility that you may have stolen them.'
> 'Son, you take some awful chances,' Henry said softly.
> 'This is a business matter, Henry, and plain talk is the best way to settle it. The pearls are only false pearls so we should very easily be able to come to an agreement. I mean you no ill will, Henry, and I am obliged to you for procuring the whisky, but business is business. Will you

take fifty dollars and return the pearls and no questions asked?'

Henry laughed shortly and mirthlessly, but he seemed to have no animosity in his voice when he said: 'So you think I stole some marbles and am sitting around here waiting for a flock of dicks to swarm me?'

This pleasant conceit rates (as Henry would say) comment on two fronts. One of its features is that this is Chandler writing himself large. Over the years he would certainly have succumbed to becoming one with the hundreds upon tens of thousand 'Britishers' in America who in the course of some social occasion have said, the better to send themselves up (and put the natives down); 'I say, old bean, high time we had the memsahib organize a spot of tiffin, wouldn'tcher say, what?' Chandler would have had the tact to play this card very seldomly but he does so here to genuinely funny effect and, suddenly, we have become conscious that Walter Gage is rather a combination of Bertie Wooster, Jeeves, Raffles and Beau Geste. Chandler here is writing in the slipstream of the boy who finished at Dulwich the year that he himself arrived – P.G. Wodehouse.

The story remains a sport because Chandler did not persevere with Walter Gage or any other of his ilk. This was surely a happy decision. The second point worthy of comment is that the premise is a one shot gag. Played over it could only have congealed into a tune on a one string fiddle – as, arguably and *pace* Hilaire Belloc, are the works of P.G. Wodehouse read large. Chandler, as I trust we shall see, would be able to work more variations within the established conventions of the straight thriller genre.

It is a historical fact that of the twenty-plus short stories by

Chandler we have, all but three to four take their place in the straightforward 'thriller' category. These, crudely, may be divided into two groups: there are the 'Good' stories and the 'Better'. Each individual reader – out of the now millions! – is likely to shuffle and divide the pack in combinations that differ slightly from his neighbour's. (What will tend to have made the difference will be the smoothness of the plotting.) But the bed-rock truth is that all of the stories are readable. And more than that. Thanks to Chandler's energy, wit and polished prose they prove lastingly re-readable. This is no small and merely 'pulp fiction' thing. Any work that is susceptible to being read with enjoyment more than once is in danger of having to be labelled 'Literature'.

In stark contrast to Walter's trailing strands of Ivy League privilege in his wake 'Pick-up on Noon Street' takes us into one of Los Angeles' 1930s mixed race areas. Consequently a number of the characters it deploys are black. They are more than 'extras'. They have speaking parts. Now, in our current times of hyper-sensitised, political correctness and race-to-race deference, it might well be considered that Noon Street be off-limits for a white writer. Such effrontery! The territory must be the preserve of a Walter Mosley. For Chandler, though, in 1936, no such inhibition prevailed. His concern was less to avoid registering as a condescending ethnic tourist than to sound authentic. As a suitable litmus test passage by which we may attempt to judge whether he succeeds in this area we might go to the exchange he renders between a black street walker and her young, flash, dandy of a hoodlum.

> 'You gotta buy liquor if you take *me* home, Smiler.'
> 'Next time, baby. I'm fresh outa dough.'

The girl's voice got hard.
'Then I tells you goodbye in the next block, handsome.'
'Like hell, baby,' the man answered.
The arc at the intersection threw light on them. They walked across the street far apart. At the other side the man caught the girl's arm.
'Listen, you cheap grafter,' she shrilled. 'Keep your paws down, see! Tinhorns are dust to me. Dangle!'
'How much liquor you gotta have, baby.'
'Plenty.'
'Me bein' on the nut, where do I collect it?'
'You got hands, ain't you?' the girl sneered. Her voice dropped the shrillness. She leaned close to him again. 'Maybe you got a gun, big boy. Got a gun?'
'Yeah. And no shells for it.'
'The goldbricks over on Central don't know that.'

Once again, long decades make it difficult to assess this for accuracy of aural observation. But while my own sustained acquaintanceship with Los Angeles is also long in the past, I find that, given the genre is in part a melodrama travelling a few inches off the ground, the exchange convinces as to authenticity. I detect no trace of Stepin Fetchit in it. The two may be dumb low-lifes but they are treated with impeccably objective indifference as regards their race.

'Blackmailers Don't Shoot' had put Chandler on the edge, at least, of his chosen map and eight months later he followed it up with 'Smart-Aleck Kill', another private eye story but one distinctly better for being more relaxed. It is still replete with tough guy gun play and a rickety plot structure but Chandler's core virtues are beginning to register their added value. He begins to score by deploying the wry humour, the sardonic acceptance, which his sharp observation of the material world allows him to imply about human nature.

> There was a grilled door and a man behind it who had given up trying to look as if it mattered who came in.

Not in a night club but on the Clapham Bus, we can all identify with that.

But it is not just a matter of slick one-liners. Chandler's writing has acquired functional economy and rhythmical elegance. The following paragraph, a necessary moment of scene-setting, is essentially just a list. But the items in the list are chosen with an impressionistic painter's expertise to give us a sense of the whole and there is just enough variation in the rhythm of the sentences to prevent the paragraph becoming monotonous.

> Black and silver curtains opened in an inverted V against a haze of cigarette and cigar smoke. The brasses of the dance band shot brief flashes of colour through the haze. There was a smell of food and liquor and perfume and face powder. The dance floor was an empty splash of amber light and looked slightly larger than a screen star's bath mat.

We know exactly where we are. And the final disenchanted wise-crack – another early example of Chandler's use of simile – tells us exactly what wavelength we need to be tuned to as we read on.

Chandler, in any case, was writing on. His third pulp success, published in late 1934, was a further improvement still – so much so, I think, that it can be described as a quantum leap in his career. 'Finger Man' is the first Chandler work to introduce us to one Philip Marlowe. And it is the first of his stories to employ the device of subjective, first-person narration. The implications of this – indeed, the end results – were to prove defining. They require considered analysis. But since where Chandler turned to his first full-length novel he chose to revisit 'Finger Man' and re-work material from it into *The Big Sleep*, I prefer to delay discussing his change in narrative stance until later. Suffice it to say for the moment that, come the mid-1930s, Chandler had found his best key signature.

This did not, however, see him slavishly reprising his newly found formula. The stories of the next five years made use of varying protagonists and voices. That trying on for size of a cultivated and literate, East Coast Beau Geste persona, remember, was to come only as late as 1939, a year which saw the publication of another Chandler story standing somewhat apart from his general succession of guys coming through doors with guns in their hands.

Probably because, atypically, it appeared in *The Saturday Evening Post*, 'I'll Be Waiting' is shorter than other Chandler stories and far less explicitly violent. The gun play is made to take place off stage. The suspense element is also downplayed. Exhibiting a classic unity of time and place, 'I'll Be Waiting' is primarily a mood piece. Chandler sets time and, right at the outset, place with an apparently effortless grace.

> At one o'clock in the morning, Carl, the night porter, turned down the last of three table lamps in the main lobby of the Windermere Hotel. The blue carpet darkened a shade or two and the walls drew back into remoteness.

In the corners were memories like cobwebs. Tony Reseck yawned.

Tony Reseck's occupation is one Chandler had a soft spot for. He is the hotel detective. But although a detective of a sort, Reseck is not the investigator here or the catalyst of what is about to transpire. He is largely a by-standing observer. One guest in the hotel is a beautiful, somehow lost, girl whom Reseck might allow himself to love were he not unprepossessingly middle-aged and fat. Another guest, just booked in, is the man, a few days out of San Quentin, who is the girl's ex-husband. They are here to hook up again. But outside the hotel is a black car and guys with guns. They believe the ex-convict owes them. They are here to collect. One of these guys is an Al Reseck, Tony's brother. Good brother, bad brother. Not all bad. Hell, family is family. Al gets to Tony and tells him to get the girl out of harm's way. Instead, trying to save him, Tony sets about smuggling the marked man to safety. It doesn't work. In that same lobby he receives a phone call. The ex-convict has been shot dead. So has Tony's brother. The tragedy has happened just out of sight but in a long dying fall we share its impact on the character who has commanded our sympathy.

> The phone clicked dryly, like a pebble hitting a wall.
> Tony put the phone down in its cradle carefully, so as not to make any sound. He looked at the clenched palm of his left hand. He took a handkerchief out and rubbed the palm softly and straightened the fingers out with his other hand. Then he wiped his forehead. The clerk came around the screen again and looked at him with glinting eyes.

'I'm off Friday. How about lending me that phone number?'

Tony nodded at the clerk and smiled a minute frail smile. He put his handkerchief away and patted the pocket he had put it in. He turned and walked away from the desk, across the entrance lobby, down the three shallow steps, along the shadowy reaches of the main lobby, and so in through the arch to the radio room once more. He walked softly, like a man moving in a room where someone is very sick. He reached the chair he had sat in before and lowered himself into it inch by inch. The girl slept on motionless, in that curled-up looseness achieved by some women and all cats. Her breath made no slightest sound against the vague murmur of the radio.

Tony Reseck leaned back in the chair and clasped his hands on his elk's tooth and quietly closed his eyes.

According to his correspondence Chandler had grave misgivings both during the writing of 'I'll Be Waiting' and after its completion as to its inherent worth. He felt at times it was rubbish; at others that it distinctly seemed to achieve what he sought. He need not have worried. Beyond, just possibly a couple of overly precious strainings – it would be better without the Toscanini reference – 'I'll Be Waiting' is indeed an achievement. What its dying fall rounds off for us is the muted atmosphere of place, the sense of tamped down emotion that Chandler's carefully modulated and distanced prose has been subtly conjuring from the start. This is a story echoing the still, sad music of a humanity lost in the melodramatic consequences of a pulp fiction existence. It is his gloss on the vanity of human wishful-thinkingness. And it is through the quality of the words, there locally in succession on the page, that he achieves this impression.

Readers of pulp fiction in the 1930s must have been grateful for the emergence of Raymond Chandler. He first published just as Dashiell Hammett, broken down by alcohol and finished off by retrospective horror at what he had endured putting in an uninterrupted, thirty-hour, dead-line beating stint to complete *The Glass Key*, threw in the towel. Devotees ever since have been at (needless) odds as to which of the two writers is finally the better. Hammett's advocates are wedded to his inflexibly Spartan mind-set and prose. Things happen one after another. No frills, sweetheart. The sentences unfold across the page with the regularity of box-cars clanking by on a coast-to-coast freight as Hammett scrupulously depersonalizes his own Continental Operator protagonist. Strictly business, ma'am. No glamour. No charisma. Just the hard-boiled facts.

Well, not entirely. Under strictest analytical scrutiny Chandler's stories tend to divide into sheep and goats on the basis of how relatively plausible and logical their plots are. But so do Hammett's. They may be boiled diamond-hard on the surface but crack into, say, *The Golden Horseshoe* and you find that in terms of coincidence and incredibility its centre is as mushy as a marshmallow left out in the sun on a Tijuana sidewalk.

And besides: never compare writers. Only compare specific examples of their work.

An ironic but not entirely insignificant coda must be appended to an account of Raymond Chandler's career as a writer of pulp fiction. In the stories the booze flows in torrents. The heroes are coshed, drugged, shot at, framed – always the sovereign remedy is Scotch. Whisky lubricates the confrontations between the good guys and the hard man. On the edge of every scene in bar and night-spot liquor is being ordered and served. The fifth is omnipresent in Marlowe's desk drawer. But not in Chandler's own life. If his correspondence and anecdote are to be believed he spent the eight or so years from 1932 onward imposing a personal Prohibition on himself. During this time he and Cissy lived lives financially straitened and modest to the point of seclusion. It was now, indeed, as if in lieu of a helter-skelter social life, that Chandler began building up the enormous correspondence – with other authors, publishers, agents, fans, Tom Cobley – that he persisted with for the rest of his life. That he could remain so steadfastly on the wagon while putting a drink in the hand of so many of his characters demonstrates that for a while, at least, he was able to exercise a will of iron.

It was all to change and utterly. By the late 1930s Chandler had become the author of choice in the *Black Mask* stable. He had acquired an agent. The agent approached the major New York publisher Alfred Knopf, about the possibility of their commissioning a full-length Chandler novel. A hardback. A proper book. Knopf sailed for the idea. Well into his fifties by now, Chandler was about to enter into that more leisurely and spacious kingdom for which his talents were best suited and where they might thus best find their fullest expression.

The Big Sleep

PUBLISHED IN 1939, RAYMOND CHANDLER'S FIRST novel-length thriller, *The Big Sleep*, turned over a modest profit for Knopf but was no big thing. It was to take the emergence of the Hawks' film version – a considerably, even substantially different, hill of beans – to bring the book's author high profile attention and acclaim. The public could relate more readily, it seemed, to Sid Hickox's crisply moody lighting, Bogart's twitch and Bacall's pout than to Chandler's choicely deployed words on the page. But if so, there was poetic – or, better, prosaic – justice in his reputation now catching a ride on the movie. As we shall have cause to examine in due course, it was Chandler's input into the screenplay of the huge 1944 box-office success *Double Indemnity* that had paved the way for the classic stream of post-World War II 'noir' thrillers the Hollywood studios chiefs became happy to commission.

As ever, people saw the film and then bought the book. But by 1946 going on '47 there were four full-length Philip Marlowe novels out upon the world. People bought *The Big Sleep* and then went looking for more Chandler. Sooner rather than later the penny dropped. If they wished to go on feeding this new habit, they would have to go back in time. They would need to revert to the short stories Chandler had produced in the 1930s.

This, I suggest, is the almost universal pattern. The reader, common or otherwise, discovers Chandler at full length and only comes upon the earlier short fiction at a later reading stage. This is of rather small consequence, no doubt, and possibly equates rather directly, give or take, with the way we become acquainted with the wider works, including the juvenilia, of such varied writers as Ford Madox Ford, say, Anthony Powell, William Trevor, Jean Rhys. But in Chandler's case, this return to yesterday serves to underline a major fact of literary genesis: Chandler's first novels are derived in very direct line of structural descent from his published short fiction.

This is palpably the case with the very first of all. The briefest pause for recollection confirms that *The Big Sleep* is a deft dovetailing of the (modified) plot-lines of the 1935 'Killer in the Rain' and the 1936 'The Curtain'. The full-length novel resulting from this fusion breaks down on analysis into three near equal but interleaved sections – narrative derived from the two original short stories and a third element made up of mint new incident and prose. A cynic, therefore, might feel that there is an immediate case for arguing that presented by Knopf with the opportunity to graduate to hardcover status, Chandler chose the line that would offer the minimum resistance to the consolidation of his career among the ranks of 'respectable' authors.

I dare say there is something to this. Chandler would have been well aware of what had caught Knopf's eye in the first place.

He would have been anxious to deliver more of the same. Further, by his own admission, he found plotting difficult: to revisit would have seemed easier than to invent entirely. At the lowest level of cunning, part of Chandler's brain may have been urging him that the folks who bought dime novels were not the people who forked out for hardbacks. And even if there were a few who read both sides of the street, scarcely a one would remember what specific hoops the unidentified narrator of 'Killer in the Rain' or John Carmody, the private eye in 'The Curtain', were made to jump through.

As the enduring status of the end product in question makes very plain, however, to argue thus is to do Chandler a huge disservice. And he, if he chose to be utterly precious, might seize the high ground by counter-arguing: what about Handel, Rembrandt, Monet, Herrick, Hokusai, Hawks? There is a type of creative artist whose cast of mind compels a constant returning to a narrowly defined point of (re)departure in the hopeless, the sublime, wish *this* time to achieve perfection. Well, Chandler, as he (almost) well knew, was no Rembrandt. But he was serious artist enough to know when improvement could be made to his own work: and here, with the Knopf contract, was opportunity to refine and, writing larger where the *Black Mask* straitjacket had required him to write small, enhance.

His artistic conscience could be clear on this. It was not going to be his intention crudely and cheaply to 'cut' and 'paste' (as in our post-electronic revolution age we now put it) a full-length work of Frankensteinesque approximation to the genuine article. His aesthetic acumen had informed him that writing at full novel length would allow him to play to perhaps his greatest strength. The greater amplitude of the novel, its extended wavelength, if you like, would allow him to deploy the facility with which his Dulwich education and a half lifetime of reading the classics had endowed him. He knew that he could write gracefully turned and cadenced prose whose variedly controlled use of subordinate clauses, interfacing with sharp dialogue, employment of pungent metaphor and *mot juste* adjectives could tell a tale in a way that would hold a worthwhile reader's attention at least as well as the slam-bang short sentencing of pure pulp. Prose – words interactively evolving one after the other line by line on his page – was always the alpha as well as the omega of Chandler's work. We know from his letters that, when in some of the later novels he had painted himself into a corner he did not clamp an ice-pack on his head and, Wilkie Collins fashion, construct convoluted yet ultra-detailed plot outlines. Instead he went back to page one and waiting to see where the lines would take him made a new beginning. (Writing, indeed life, might have been easier for him if he had possessed a touch of Collins and his books might have been tighter in terms of cause and effect. But if the increment of Collins had been at the expense of a diminution of Chandler, the resulting fiction would not have been as good.) In sitting down to 'construct' *The Big Sleep* Chandler also went back to the first line on the first page. Though he took incident after incident from the two source stories, he reworked every paragraph in turn on a line-by-line basis. He now had scope to enlarge, refine, add further effect, add sub-text.

As regards the conjoining of 'Killer in the Rain' with 'The Curtain', Chandler's carpentry was thoroughly smooth. He made the blackmail victim of the first story the second's prime murderer. Great benefit immediately ensued. In 'The Curtain' the original killer proved to be a psychotic brat of a child in a Los Angeles household with massively more money and influence than collective sense or morality. The child is a boy scarcely on the edge of puberty but, spoiled rotten by his rotten environment, quite capable of killing if not indulged. His mother is a rackety socialite, man-hungry in a desultory way, divorced and idle-rich directionless. In *The Big Sleep*, however, Chandler converts the boy into a teenage girl, as essentially, is her predecessor in 'Killer in the Rain'. She has no more a mental age and sense of right and wrong than the boy did but she is a character in motion. The boy is passive. He is still, in everyday terms, liable to be told to go and wash behind his ears. He can't drive a car. The girl can. Carmen Sternwood thus becomes a loose cannon within *The Big Sleep*'s plot structure. Her inanely misconceived efforts to get out from under the blackmailing her gamey exploits have incurred make her both a catalyst and, from Marlowe's point of view, a distraction from the main thrust of his investigation. She is a threat to herself, to others and, in particular, both sexually and otherwise, to Marlowe. Pinballing around in this fashion she brings great vitality to the narrative.

Further, by converting the mother of the psychotic boy to Carmen Sternwood's older sister, Vivian, Chandler achieves a further major refinement. Vivian remains an idle-rich socialite good-time girl who somehow cannot have a good time, but she is not all bad: in her heart of hearts she recognizes herself for what she is. Further, she is concerned to safeguard other members of the family. She recognizes the core decency beneath Marlowe's flip, tough-guy professional façade. She admires him. She admires him a lot.

Chandler makes Vivian a sexually attractive woman and, in making her a sister instead of a mother to a pubescent boy, makes her – in the context of the thriller genre – available. In due course, amid mounting external tensions, she comes on to Marlowe and he, although it is a close run thing, does not reciprocate fully in kind. He no more has sex with Vivian Sternwood than, despite given the ultimate opportunity, he has previously had with her sister. The reason he does not is part of the overall Chandler-Marlovian ethos that must receive later discussion. The immediate point is that far from crudely slam-banging two plots together regardless, Chandler has integrated them with thought-through modifications which afford a distinctly richer structural and thematic mix.

Chandler made apparent how he proposed to modulate from the minor to the major key with the first sentence of his first novel-length work of fiction.

> It was about eleven o'clock in the morning, mid-October, with the sun not shining and a look of hard wet rain in the clearness of the foothills.

There is no roscoe spitting fire; no grifter brought to a shuddering halt as he realizes his last string is played out; no body on the sidewalk oozing life. There is no flashy 'hook' designed to pin the reader (and commissioning editor) to the wall at the very outset. Chandler eschews all melodrama. This measured sentence might be the beginning of any novel in The Great

Tradition. Not, however (even though there will clearly be no possibility of taking a walk that day) a Victorian novel.

The brisk, demotic vocabulary has a later ring. To indicate that it is overcast by the just-slightly-about-face 'with the sun not shining' and to describe the oncoming rain as 'hard wet' informs our subconscious receptors that this is prose downstream from early Hemingway, Dos Passos, perhaps Dawn Powell. It is a non-specific, modest plea to be noticed that might be the clearly literate prelude to a thousand and one continuations. But it does not continue with an account of troop movements beyond the further bank of the Ebro; nor with a description of a torrential storm mowing down the Ohio corn harvest. At once a subtle modulation encourages us to adjust to a more prosaic wavelength.

> I was wearing my powder blue suit, with dark blue shirt, black brogues, black wool socks with dark blue clocks on them. I was neat, clean, shaved and sober, and I didn't care who knew it. I was everything the well-dressed private detective ought to be. I was calling on four million dollars.

Ah! A private eye. We were beginning to think along those lines. A university professor, a Wall Street banker does not regard the shade of powder blue as impressively formal. In any case, there is a disarmingly unprofessorial insouciance about this character: that he openly flags up that he is spick and span and sober lets us know directly that he isn't shy about acknowledging that there are times when he's not. Nor that he has a pragmatic eye for a main chance. Four million bucks is no matter for casual dress code.

Instantly this seems to offer us more than the two-dimensional shorthand of a standard pulp. This protagonist is already being rounded out by tone of voice, detailed description, ordering of cadence into that category of 'character'.

The protagonist is swiftly progressed through entrance doors which would have let in a troop of Indian elephants into 'the main hallway of the old Sternwood place.' Interestingly, Chandler does not, as yet, let us know what part of the world we find ourselves in. He leaves us, though, in no doubt as to the nature of our immediate surroundings:

> Over the entrance doors ... there was a broad stained glass panel showing a knight in dark armour rescuing a lady who was tied to a tree and didn't have any clothes on but some very long and convenient hair. The knight had pushed the vizor of his helmet back to be sociable, and he was fiddling with the knots on the ropes that tied the lady to the tree and not getting anywhere. I stood there and thought that if I lived in the house, I would sooner or later have to climb up there and help him. He didn't seem to be really trying ...
>
> On the east side of the hall, a free staircase, tile-paved, rose to a gallery with a wrought iron railing and another piece of stained glass romance. Large hard chairs with rounded red plush seats were backed into the vacant spaces of the hall round about. They didn't look as if anybody ever sat in them. In the middle of the west wall there was a big empty fireplace with a brass screen in front of four hinged panels and over the fireplace a marble mantle with cupids in the corners.

This description (and considerably more) equates directly with the arrival of Carmody, the private eye in 'The Curtain', to the prototype mansion. But there, the description is in merely scene-setting shorthand. In *The Big Sleep* the leisurely pace is allowed to continue. We are given time to take in along with the new visitor – ah, yes, he's an investigator; he is an observant man – that although executed on a scale befitting a four-million-dollar fortune, this hallway leaves a lot to be desired. It aims, copycat fashion, for European tradition. It achieves Hollywood kitsch. It seems pleasing that the newcomer is far from overawed.

Speedily, however, he is all but overcome by climate control. He has been ushered into the presence of his client-to-be and the millionaire is kept, just, in the land of the living almost solely by the expedient of being housed alongside countless tropical flowers in a super-heated, hyper-humid greenhouse. This is a setting shared directly by both short story and novel. Shared, that is, in terms of location. Not, however, in terms of word count. In 'The Curtain' we are told:

> The air steamed. The walls and ceilings of the glasshouse dripped. In the half light enormous tropical plants spread their blooms and branches all over the place, and the smell of them was almost as over-powering as the smell of boiling alcohol.

Rather than in the instance of describing the hallway (where he reworked 'The Curtain' version completely) Chandler chose here to expand both visually and verbally from this already arresting core. (As well he did: 'all over the place' is distinctly slack).

> The air was thick, wet, steamy and loaded with the cloying smell of tropical orchids in bloom. The glass walls and roof were heavily misted and big drops of moisture splashed down on the plants. The light had an unreal

greenish colour, like light filtered through an aquarium tank. The plants filled the place, a forest of them, with nasty meaty leaves and stalks like the newly washed fingers of dead men. They smelled as overpowering as boiling alcohol under a blanket.

This is more than the working up for its own sake of a heightened memory by a writer who had spent his youth a (potential) stone's throw from Paxton's Crystal Palace. Chandler here is allowing his prose to luxuriate so as to resemble and evoke the foliage for precise symbolic reason. Even in the original version where brevity was the sole of format, he permits himself sufficient elbow room to establish the cloying, static ambiance. In *The Big Sleep*'s version he thickens the fetid brew far more, regaling us with early rank examples of what was to emerge as his signature literary device, the simile. The object of his symbolism is patent. Kept artificially alive in this unnatural environment, General Sternwood, the multi-millionaire client, is at one with these plants. If the power is switched off both he and they will die alike. He, it is plain, is as moribund as it is possible to be while still in possession of one's faculties: and they, so overpoweringly decadent in the impression they give off, broadcast their impermanence on the sunless air.

But the house, we now can be sure, has been no less symbolic in intention. It cost a fortune: but the money was spent on facile pastiche and such bad taste as Vivian Sternwood's impossibly *téléphone blanc* personal room. In every direction as far as the eye can see, something is rotten in the house of Sternwood.

There is a type of English detective story of the 'whodunnit' variety in which, it is said, the fine country house may be taken to represent in shorthand, simplistic terms, the Great Good Place which so captivated Henry James. It is a sealed, idyllic world. Then, in the form of some criminal, the serpent enters this Eden. Chaos ensues. Eventually, the crime being solved, the serpent is crushed. Harmony is restored. Paradise is regained.

The Sternwood mansion is not a Great Good Place. It has never contributed to that stylized, sterile tradition. It is not the Great Evil Place either. As *The Big Sleep* develops we see that the Sternwood household is far from being the sole source of the multifarious evils, the crimes great and small, which beset Los Angeles, and Realito and points between. But it is home to guiltily involved parties and murderously present catalysts. The General himself is no saint.

The General is old school patrician and his crippled, wasted body still has a backbone of steel. Proud blood still trickles in his veins. But the other side of old money can be a *droit de seigneur* disregard for others. The General has been a disastrous father. His two daughters have been raised spoiled rotten brats.

Moreover the money is not that old. It is oil money. Chandler knew from his own working experience what a dirty game the Californian oil boom game had been. (He was writing just a few years on from the Teapot Dome scandal.) The Sternwood money, we may be sure, arose from their being fastest with the mostest in some pretty gamey operations. Marlowe is well aware of what this home is literally and figuratively built upon.

> The Sternwoods, having moved up the hill, could no longer smell the stale sump water or the oil, but they could still look out of their front windows and see what had made them rich.

The General, for all his personal style, knows this too. He knows his money is as tainted as his parenthood has been ruinously token. This is the underlying motive which has made him say to Marlowe on their initial encounter:

> I seem to exist largely on heat, like a new born spider and the orchids are largely an excuse for the heat.

It is true. The General sits like a spider at the heart of one socially shabby, morally sordid, lethally perverse web that is now entangled with the no less seamy threads of other even more questionable species.

It may seem to be breaking an arachnid upon a wheel to analyse the first few pages of *The Big Sleep* in virtually the same compass as their own length. I do so, however, to make a point fundamental to, and universal throughout, Chandler. Working on our subconsciousnesses as we read his text for its narrative exposition, Chandler is constantly feeding us subtextual 'clues' to the moral implications of his characters' behaviour. This is to say that he writes precisely in the tradition of Jane Austen, Dickens, Henry James. The Sternwood mansion is not, indeed, the Great Good Place. But it is designed in the same spirit as was Mansfield Park. Its own Norris, ironically, is the classiest act in the whole book, but the Sternwood daughters, Vivian and Carmen are the clear-cut cousins, not many times removed of Maria and Julia Bertram.

Comparisons are by no means invariably odious. They are frequently, whether at an immediate or a subliminal level, illuminating: often they can be trenchantly amusing. From the outset of his career as a writer of short stories Chandler had made constant use of a specific literary form of comparison, the simile and he was to continue to put this predilection to telling use until the end of that, and Marlowe's career. The simile in Chandler's hands is a device to be used to indicate the moral or aesthetic of an action, an artifact, a person or persons, a situation or any combination thereof.

The hothouse description quoted above leans heavily on simile. The likening of the light to that of an aquarium is relatively predictable but Chandler lifts the curtain on a *grand guignol* extreme. The hothouse plants have 'leaves and stalks like the newly washed fingers of dead men.' (No, there is no John Webster House in Dulwich.) The plants smell 'as overpowering as boiling alcohol under a blanket.' These lurid comparisons avoid toppling over into the ridiculous on account of the exaggeratedly rank context they themselves help to conjure and work on a direct, surface, level making us mentally gag a little. But they also work subliminally. They require our subconscious to process this question. How would the narrator, Marlowe, be in a position to make those comparisons? We do not have time to pursue the thought consciously but the implication has to be that alcohol is boiled under a blanket in rooms which are reached down mean streets.

The overwhelming majority of the similes that speed Marlowe on his way are set in less overheated more everyday contexts. Sometimes they are functionally apt through their straightforwardness. Norris, for example, the Sternwood butler, has a back 'as straight as an ironing board.' But every so often the similes are leavened by and sharpened by the element of cynical wit in the juxtaposition of their elements and by the droll dryness of the delivery. Harry Jones, the suicidedly heroic little man who is out of his league would hardly weigh as much as a 'butcher's thumb' and has eyes that 'wanted to look hard and looked as hard as oysters on the half shell.' Vivian Sternwood's *télélephone blanc* room is 'a screenstar's boudoir, a place of charm and seduction, artificial as a wooden leg.' Cronjoyer, a senior, by-the-book cop is 'a cold-eyed hatchet-faced man, as lean as a rake and as hard as the manager of a loan office.'

Chandler, as we began by saying, had no compunction about pouring plot-lines into new bottles. But he was happy to recycle titbits too. Not only 'Killer in the Rain' and 'The Curtain' are reprocessed in *The Big Sleep* but, fleetingly, Chandler's very first pulp story 'Blackmailers Don't Shoot'. I have already discussed how in the course of its telling Rhonda Farr's eyes come to look like 'the prelude to a scream'. This second time of usage Chandler forsakes oblique, convoluted, compression for direct and non-distracting terseness. Vivian Sternwood, one on one with Marlowe, realizes that he has disinterred the one family skeleton she wanted to keep closeted away.

> For a brief instant her face seemed to come to pieces, to become merely a set of features without form or control. Her mouth looked like the prelude to a scream.

It is arresting writing. The retrieval expedition down memory lane was well justified.

At key moments, indeed, the similes are put to deeper use than providing on-the-fly impressions. Chandler does a brilliant job of making Carmen Sternwood appear as credibly sub-human, witlessly psychotic and ferally vicious as an at-first-glance sexily attractive teenager could possibly be. He begins to key in how damagingly flawed she is right at the outset of the book when Marlowe first meets her.

> She came over near me and smiled with her mouth and she had little sharp predatory teeth, as white as fresh orange pith and as shiny as porcelain.

Although Carmen Sternwood's own, the teeth are somehow as artificial as a wooden leg without the laughs.

Towards the further end of the book Chandler uses a simile to pin down a human experience better, I feel, than any other writer has managed. Marlowe stands in the night and the rain outside a remote building in which he knows lurks very genuine dangers. He has to go in. He bangs on the door. The immediate upshot is that 'there was a hung instant of silence, as heavy as thunder.' A simple use of words. And yet the force of the instant being 'hung', the compression of 'heavy as thunder' – i.e. like the heaviness that is in the air when a thunderstorm is imminent – encapsulates a sensation which we have all experienced when under pressure and fearful that we have triggered a dire consequence.

In Marlowe's case dire consequences do ensue and he is knocked unconscious. As he begins to come around he finds that he is 'trussed like a turkey ready for the oven' and still feeling woozy from concussion. It is at this point that Chandler graces his text with a near simile he should have been allowed to patent.

> Overhead the rain still pounded, with a remote sound, as if it was somebody else's rain.

Once in a very rare while a Chandler simile misfires through trying too hard. Thus, as he closes in on a dangerous killer,

Chandler finds himself back at the Sternwood mansion. It is a sunny day and he is in the spacious grounds. But there is danger in the air and Chandler wishes to prefigure the fact. Thus he writes:

> The sunshine was as empty as a head waiter's smile.

This doesn't work. It doesn't work because Chandler is trying to yoke together two elements too far removed to stand even a quirkily apt comparison. Sunlight is universal, external, bucolic, impersonal. A head waiter is individual, internal, metropolitan, human. The attempt to fuse the two comes over as strained. It makes us feel that Chandler is trying to exact revenge for umbrage given in an LA eatery the night before.

A lot has been said about Chandler's ear as regards the cadencing, the wise-cracking timing of the simile. Perhaps not enough notice has been taken of the sharpness of his eye. A simile compares this with that. To make the comparison, you need to observe a connection or, of course, a significant non-connection. Marlowe, as Norris immediately perceives, notices detail because he earns his living as a detective. Chandler clearly observed things too. The artist Samuel Palmer shrewdly said of the simile in an essay that it 'at once enriches the subject matter by analogies, and, as opposites manifest each other, enforces it by a contrast.' Chandler was an exponent of the device because he was in two senses a man of action. A man who can write 'he looked at me the way a horse looks at you over a fence' has clearly gone about the world with both his eyes and his mind open. And indeed the gracefully functional descriptions of landscapes, buildings, shorelines against which Chandler occasionally sets his action testify to how open those eyes steadily were. It is the visual acuity – sunlight and headwaiters always excepted – informing Chandler's similes that gives them their aptness. But then, as he had long since known, this is true of Homer also.

Encapsulating, signposting, summarizing, pinpointing a minor character or confirming a moral attitude in a sentence, Chandler's similes gift his narrative with steady increments to its momentum. They let Chandler get on with things. As does Marlowe.

Leaving the mephitic decadence of the Sternwood hothouse he goes down the hill into the real world (in terms of the thriller genre) of what has emerged to be Los Angeles and gets on the case. In due course establishing that the 'missing person' conundrum and the blackmailing attempt are obliquely linked he up-to-a-point delivers.

Two killers, both psychotic but otherwise very different, have been taken out of circulation. One, a murderously sadistic criminal has been outwitted and out-gunned by Marlowe. ('I couldn't wait ... long enough to be a gentleman of the old school.') The other not finally responsible for her actions has been routed towards the best psychiatric treatment that money can buy. A blackmailing pornographer has been hoist on the skuzzy petard of his own proclivity. Through her acquaintanceship with Marlowe and her growing respect for his qualities, General Sternwood's flaky older daughter has been brought in touching distance of her own redemption. But there is a debit side to the ledger too.

In the course of Marlowe's investigation half a dozen lesser characters are done to unnatural death – not all of them, by any means, meeting with their just deserts. The most thorough-going criminal to whom we have been introduced, Eddie Mars, an archetypal Mr Big, walks away from all of the crime scenes scot-free clearly – this is not the film! – living to fight another blackmailing day. And Marlowe's discovery that Sternwood's missing surrogate son, Rusty Regan, has long since been murdered leaves perhaps the bitterest taste of all. The news is too sad to pass on to the old man. Marlowe may have wriggled off the police hook as regards the four shots he ungentlemanly pumped into Eddie Mars' low-life 'best boy' but the General will have to remain lying quiet in his canopied bed with his bloodless hands folded on the sheet, his heart a brief, uncertain murmur, his thoughts as grey as ashes as he waits for, what else, but the big sleep.

When laid out on a slab in the Literary Morgue *The Big Sleep* exhibits no few blemishes to the coldly cast eye. The removal of two minor characters from the initial cat's-cradling mix by means of the perpetrating of two identical *crimes passionnels* is slack repetition. (The subsequent death of one is infamously obscure as Howard Hawks bore witness to. Did the boy chauffeur fixated on Carmen Sternwood smash the family Packard through fencing into the Pacific by accident or by suicidal intent? Or was he pushed?) That Harry Jones and the worthless dame he worships chance while out driving to clock the key witness who links the two major plot lines is a convenience too facile to stand up when subjected to cold-blooded analysis.

But none of these carping, wise after the reading, criticisms really matter. We don't read in cold blood. What truly matters is the concept of the two guys with guns coming through the door to keep the foreground action tense and sweaty. It is not important whether the Sternwood chauffeur's death was accident, suicide or murder. What counts is that the aftermath gives Chandler a nice, moody scene and a chance to work in some police procedure. Yes, it is indeed a stretch – a big stretch – that quite by chance Harry Jones is enabled to tail Eddie Mars' wife and Rusty Reagan's mistress to her hideaway. But the momentum generated by the novel's pace allows us to swallow it down in one. In our eagerness to discover what will happen next we breeze right past the blemish. And the convenience is as nothing compared to the convoluted coincidences of ten thousand other story lines; of, say, *A Tale of Two Cities*. If we can blink but then pass over the enormity of Darnley being a scion of the St Evrémonde family, Chandler is home free.

There is an aspect of *The Big Sleep* that seventy-five years on from its writing must perhaps be considered a more serious and lasting blemish. In its early stage it sounds a subdued but distinct homophobic note. Geiger, the pornographer-blackmailer, is a homosexual. He is killed in a fit of red-misted rage on account of his activities and not his nature. But there is a distinct tang of 'good riddance' over his thus being eliminated. Marlowe, who never stoops to four-letter swear words, does unhesitatingly make use of 'queer' and 'faggot'.

The morning after Geiger's murder Marlowe revisits the victim's home, scene of the crime. Its decor, its fixtures and fittings are unashamedly, as we might now say, camp. Marlowe, apparently with straightforward distaste says: 'all this in the daytime had a stealthy nastiness like a fag party.' We are bound on reflection, are we not, to ask: how would Marlowe come to know about the ambiance of a homosexual's entertaining? How, for that matter, would Chandler?

Similarly, when Geiger's live-in punk boyfriend exacts a knee jerk and desperately misconceived lover's revenge on the man he thinks responsible for Geiger's death, Chandler depicts him, arrested now by Marlowe, with withering lack of respect. His only utterance is a single phrase obscenity endlessly repeated. He is the most dehumanized character Chandler ever drew.

The homosexual relationship between the Fat Man, Gutman, and Joel Cairo which Dashiell Hammett clearly indicates in *The Maltese Falcon* does not strike me as spiteful. Its purpose seems more to endow them with a further layer of exotic, alien, otherness. The pair are the more sinister for being the more *outré*. Is it contemporary political correctness raised to the level of irrelevant absurdity to comment that in *The Big Sleep* the fact that Geiger and his lover are homosexuals seems to come very close to being offered as justification all of itself for their receiving their comeuppances? Thus, a deeper question arises. We may have to ask ourselves whether since, *autre temps, autre moeurs*, Chandler is simply playing to the prejudices of those with eyes sufficiently open and wits enough to catch, nudge, nudge, his drift. Or might it be that, in employing this contemptuously dismissive, homophobic tone, he is so letting down his guard as to be caught protesting too much? Let the question abide until room for a spacious reckoning becomes available.

Philip Marlowe

IN INVITING HIM TO STEP UP from the *Black Mask* bush league to the full-length, hardback majors, Alfred Knopf was requiring Raymond Chandler to raise his game and re-align his sights. Chandler responded by moving up through the gears with a smooth intelligence. Integral to this response was the adoption of what we may call a literally page-one narrative attitude. He opted for recounting his story in the first person from the viewpoint of his central protagonist. As in his magazine work that protagonist was to be a private eye. The name was Marlowe.

This basic device raises an immediate issue so obvious as almost not to require comment but, for that very reason, does need addressing. In making the action hero his narrator Chandler, at a stroke, was depriving himself of the ultimate down-beat or totally *noir* ending. If we exclude all possibility – as with Chandler we should – of a tricksy *Murder of Roger Ackroyd* denouement or a death cell confession/deathbed testimony format, then by narrative definition Marlowe is inevitably bound to be alive as the story concludes. He may be a sadder and no wiser man, he may be disillusioned. He may feel himself diminished. But he is still standing and able to tell his tale. The one card Chandler cannot deal his hero is the Ace of Spades.

In reading practice, however, this scarcely seems to matter. Chandler is skilful enough in having Marlowe sapped, drugged, beaten up, framed and shot at along his tortuous way to tighten our attention every time those two guys with guns in their hands come through the door. Our pulses do race. We do grip the book more tightly.

All of this is obvious. I make laborious matter of it now to anticipate a later discussion. Marlowe's status *vis à vis* the overall structure of the novels he narrates impacts critically upon their own status within the *noir* canon.

More immediately the first-person narration prompts a subtler consideration: when an author employs the pronoun 'I' as his channel of observation, exposition and comment, the distinction between writer and protagonist may become blurred to the point of complete coalescence. To its huge detriment Proust's *Recherche* is virtually an autobiography. Jane Eyre, for better or worse, is frequently Charlotte Bronte's wishful thinking. Robinson Crusoe, however, is not Daniel Defoe. Neither, given the violent, larger than life, travelling off the ground melodrama of the thriller genre, can Marlowe possibly be Chandler. But the character and his author are first cousins.

What forges this relationship links back to the quality of the prose. If Chandler wished to play to his 'literary' strength and write prose at times elegantly sinuous, at others trenchantly ironic, prose carefully crafted in its varying cadences so as to place emphasis on the key word, prose regularly interspersed with pungent, crackling, colloquial dialogue exchange – if Chandler was to seek to deploy his words on the page to achieve such effects and do so in the first-person form, it follows as night follows day, as a gumshoe follows his mark, that he must endow his protagonist with a large measure of his own sensibilities.

Chandler had already put the name Philip Marlowe to use when introducing him to *Black Mask* readers as early as 1934 in that subsequently *Big Sleep*-cannibalized 'Finger Man'. But Marlowe there is essentially one with other of his private eye heroes whether first- or third-person protagonists – Mallory, Dalmas, Carmody. Straitjacketed by the space constraints of the pulp they are all pretty much of a stereotypical muchness: straight shooting, toughly honourable, wise-cracking, two-fistedly handsome, intelligent enough, aware of the correct knife to eat their peas off.

Entering now in 1938 upon the greater amplitude not only offered but demanded by the full-length novel, Chandler needed more than a stereotype. This Philip Marlowe was to be the guide, the eyes leading us through the narrative. He needed to be the observing eyes, the sensitive observer. He needed to be sufficiently intelligent and articulate to convey to the reader the import of what he saw and what he felt. So as to add spice to the mix he would need to be a wittily ironic, even cynical man with a tongue capable of encapsulating that wit in a smart crack, a sharp put down. Chandler's previous short-term heroes had all been capable of cracking wise: but usually when braced by the cops or confronted by Mr Big. In the proposed *Big Sleep* that Chandler was evolving in his mind, much of the dialogue would be between Marlowe and the reader. Much of the exposition would emerge as if Marlowe were sitting across from the reader as they nursed drinks in a booth in a quiet bar. Alternatively, if Marlowe is a latter-day knight errant questing through the wild modern urban woods, we as the reader, become the faithful squire at his side. This gives us a privileged position because we become the first beneficiary of Marlowe's otherwise private thoughts. If the narratives were written in the third person, Marlowe's wry, world-weary, disgusted or whatever *subjective* takes on all he encounters and sees would go by the board. In making Marlowe his mouthpiece Chandler hit upon the perfect vehicle for his commentating purpose.

And, most crucially of all, this enlarged and rounded out Marlowe would be not only a witty man but a man with moral sensibilities too. He would have a personal integrity. He would have contempt for corrupt politicians and crooked cops. He would believe you could fight City Hall – that you should. A realist-cum-fatalist, he might not believe that you should ever expect to win such a war. But honour compelled you to try and maybe you'd be able to pull off a few pyrrhic defeats.

It all thus comes together. With Marlowe the style is the man and the style is Chandler's and it is his prose style that gives us Marlowe.

To spell the above out is perhaps to cross the border into parody. But I feel it necessary. It is this nexus of author's style and sensibility and protagonist narrator's viewpoint which most differentiates Chandler from his most distinguished pulp predecessor. Although addressing us in the first person Hammett's Continental Op, anonymous, uncharismatic, is not lollygagging away in the back of an amiable bar. He is unfolding his evidence, fact upon chronological fact, to a court of inquiry. Facts are impersonal; so is the Op's tone. It is free from any editorializing embroidery. With a Puritan zeal, a Puritan refusal to display a trace of gusto Hammett rigidly adheres to the deliberately flat monotone he believes best serves the passage of the narrative. When he too expanded his storytelling into novel-length work he essentially eschewed deviating from this one-note deadpan rehearsal of fact after fact, incident after incident. We are left to infer all but the most prosaic adverbs. It is this stoical refusal to meet his readers halfway which earns Hammett his most dedicated admirers. Because, however, Chandler's protagonist, far from being an anonymous conduit to the facts, has a personality and embodies certain human values – honour, compassion, cynicism, a sense of obligation – it is necessary for him to editorialise as his narrative unfolds. Marlowe never gives us sustained analyses of how the facts he is unravelling appear to stack up – we are spared those bore-you-to-death interim summaries that bedevil such so crudely inferior works as James Ellroy's *LA Confidential* – but he does describe to us not only the settings and the events, but also the personalities he encounters as he investigates. These characters, major or minor, take on definition as refracted through his comments. We are able to begin judging these not just by their actions, as in Hammett, but through Marlowe's own (inner) running commentary. This is how he gives Agnes, the irredeemably bimbo-esque 'sales-assistant' at the phony *Big Sleep* bookstore her quietus. At first she has a certain interest for Marlowe.

> She got up slowly and swayed towards me in a tight black dress that didn't reflect any light. She had long thighs

and she walked with a certain something I hadn't often
seen in bookstores. She was an ash blonde with greenish
eyes, beaded lashes, hair waved smoothly back from ears
in which large jet buttons glittered. Her fingernails were
silvered. In spite of her get up she looked as if she would
have a hall bedroom accent.

Speedily, after Marlowe had thrown her a couple of academic flim-flam, curve-ball questions his growing impression is confirmed.

Her smile was now hanging by its teeth and eyebrows
and wondering what it would hit when it dropped.

Hammett would never have permitted himself so attention-drawing an exaggeration as this last sentence. Nor would he have intruded the personalising note that 'a certain something I hadn't often seen in bookstores' gives the initial description. But Chandler can do this because he has established Marlowe as an individual – an individual whom we have come to accept not only occasionally goes into bookstores but frequently goes out for his verbal shots. We trust his judgements. Whatever the hyperbole we are thoroughly convinced of the key fact: there is a 'vacant' sign nailed permanently in place between Agnes' greenish eyes.

Marlowe reacts varyingly and on an *ad hoc* basis with the variety of individuals with whom his investigations bring him into contact. He forms relationships, fleeting, occasionally intimate, differing one from another but all on that personal level the Continental Op assiduously avoids entering into. This is why with Chandler the ironies he draws our attention to are also personal and local. The man-mountain hoodlum turns to mush in the eminently suitable for a latter-day righter of wrongs – even if, rather than climbing a ladder to join his knight template in a stained glass window, it is his destiny to perambulate down mean streets.

Whither, in due course, we must follow.

Farewell, My Lovely

SOME HALF A DOZEN YEARS OR so after the appearance of the books in question Raymond Chandler wrote a letter to a Canadian journalist-admirer which offered a brief, casual indication of how he himself rated them:

> I believe *Farewell, My Lovely* – would be called the best of my books. *The High Window* the worst, but I have known people who would pick any of them as against the others. In some ways my last [*The Little Sister*], not yet published, is the best. But I'll never again equal *The Big Sleep* for pace nor *Farewell, My Lovely* for plot complication. I probably don't want to; the time comes when you have to choose between pace and depth of focus, between action and character, menace and wit. I now chose the second in every case.

Writing the way he did write did not come easily to Chandler. Self-confessedly he could suffer the tortures of the damned wrestling with his plotting and layering in his local effects.

Consequently his assessment of his various novels somewhat seems to be less than objective. In retrospect he may have tended to hold grudges not based purely on aesthetics against the titles that had given him more grief in their composition. Albeit that nobody else could better see their weaknesses, his 'placing' of them does hint at being influenced by the amount of blood, sweat and tears which they respectively cost him. For us, on the other disinterested hand, it doesn't at all follow that the harder they came, the poorer they were.

That said, pace is a quality able to be judged fairly objectively. Certainly *The Big Sleep*, the first noted, is the paciest. And certainly, better plotted, *Farewell, My Lovely* did follow with a change – a beneficial change – of pace. Not hugely but perceptibly it is more discursive.

It does not, of course, present us with a change in genre. It does not even represent a significant change in the Chandleresque genre. But – there is a slight change of key, a modulation. Most evidently this arises out of the increase in that bantering tone – bantering with the reader – that Marlowe already showed a tendency towards in *The Big Sleep*.

Like the first novel *Farewell, My Lovely* is essentially constructed by courtesy of the labour-saving convenience – let us not forget the second book has long been considered the toughest nut to crack in an author's progress – of fusing the plots of two of the pulp short-stories – 'Try The Girl' (1937) and 'Mandarin's Jade' (1937) – together by the simple device of endowing a single central character with two basic plot premises. Marlowe sets out to establish what these premises are (i.e. solve the case) in his usual mode. He offers us a great amount of first-person but impersonal narrative and description and exposition. He cracks wise in edgy dialogue with the hoods and the police. He gives us his slant, usually sardonic and disillusioned, on the characters he encounters and the places he visits. But now, as well, not frequently but more than when we originally met him, he sits down one-on-one opposite us in that booth and gives us an insight into how he is feeling inside his own self right here and now. Such an instance occurs when, having instantly discerned that the best way to loosen the slatternly and pathetically sordid Mrs Florian's tongue is to ply her with booze, Marlowe suits his action to his plan.

> A white look smeared the woman's face. She pushed the bottle against her lips and gurgled at it. Some of the whisky ran down her chin.
> 'And the cops are looking for *him*,' she said, and laughed. 'Cops. Yah!'
> A lovely old woman. I liked being with her. I liked getting her drunk for my own sordid purposes, I was a swell guy. I enjoyed being me. You find almost anything under your hand in my business, but I was beginning to be a little sick at my stomach.

The first paragraph is pure narrative description. And the Continental Op would consider that it says it all. He would never deign to regale us with the second paragraph. This is not narrative. It is confession. Chandler/Marlowe sitting across from us in the booth and letting the sour memory hang out. Naturally, as commentary, it slows the narrative pace. But it adds dimension to the Marlowe character. We understand why he is queasy. He is queasy because he is essentially moral. And vulnerable to his better nature. He is one of us. We like him for that. We like him even more because he is willing to take us into his confidence.

His occasional confidential tone, then, enables us to empathise with the 'everyman' in Marlowe: but it can also operate in an almost entirely opposite way. Because we are buddies Marlowe can make as if we have been around the same tracks as he. A corpse lies in a lonely place.

> He lay smeared to the ground, on his back, at the base of a bush, in that bag-of-clothes position that always means the same thing.

This is good, tense, 'noir', thriller prose. It hustles knowingly along. It all hangs on the demonstrative 'that' which operates as a nudge and a wink. 'It's one of these, old buddy,' it says. 'You and I have seen it all before.' But, in fact, inference is close to nonsense. Vivid as it is 'bag of clothes' need not at all be visually synonymous with a corpse. It could in isolation be a tarp fallen from a pick-up, a bin-liner, a heap of top soil. In this specific instance because we are aware we are reading a thriller, because the paragraph begins with 'He lay ...', because Marlowe has just been sapped unconscious, we know that this is a body. But what makes the phrase work is the familiarity that has been established between Marlowe and ourselves. In using the word 'that' Chandler confers authority not only upon the description but upon his detective and, flatteringly, upon us.

Knowing that the intimacy he has created around Marlowe makes it possible, Chandler uses the 'we're already familiar with this' formula of the demonstrative pronoun ('It had the look of ... there was that sound of ...') at select times to draw us into this flattering bond of complicity. Simultaneously, however, the device is providing another benefit of at least equal importance. The fiction of common experience between Marlowe and the reader allows Chandler to telescope description and explanation and so maintain narrative speed.

The usage of 'that' with its assumption of shared knowledge is, of course, a species of compressed simile. Thus 'in that bag of clothes position' unpacks to give us 'he lay looking like a bag of clothes'. As in *The Big Sleep* and as was to be the case in all the novels yet to come, Chandler makes *Farewell, My Lovely* replete with similes. As before, as still to come, they divide loosely into three categories. There are the quiet similes that are effective in their instant, unassuming aptness. A pregnant, communal silence, for instance, is 'as heavy as a water-logged boat,' and the 'eighty-five cent dinner tasted like a discarded mailbag.' There are then the intentionally exaggerated similes – 'she had eyes like old sins'; 'she had a face like a bucket of mud' – where, because of the wit or shock in the exaggeration we not only get the picture loud and clear, we also appreciate Marlowe's reaction, be it of contempt, admiration, lust or whatever, to the stimulus. The exaggeration further humanises him. He is not only observant and moral, he is properly discerning. And has a way with words.

Very, very occasionally – as I have argued above in the instance of the head waiter's smile in *The Big Sleep*, discernment deserts Chandler/Marlowe. The intended comparison is almost literally too far-fetched and, rejecting it we find ourselves brought up short concentrating on the local failure rather than the ongoing narrative. There is an arguable example of this right at the outset of *Farewell, My Lovely*. The outsize, outlandish Moose Malloy (a pause, please to pay silent respect to Mike Mazurki) has wandered into the decorously and authentically described black neighbourhood of Central Avenue. Chandler describes him as seeming 'as inconspicuous as a tarantula on a slice of angel food.' Well, it is better than saying that he stood out like a sore thumb. But logic is against the simile working. Very well: the root intellectual concept is incongruity, granted. But in terms of visual impression upon the inner eye the comparison is less than apt. Malloy is white: tarantulas are black. Malloy is a bulldozer of a man: tarantulas are vulnerably spindly. Tarantulas kill by scuttling stealth and speed: Malloy kills like an avalanche. In love with the sensational basic image, Chandler has over-reached.

I am inclined to think, indeed, that in *Farewell, My Lovely* and irrespective of whether individually they are good, bad or inconspicuous, Chandler overreaches in general in his use of simile. He runs a gamut from A to A via Z. In time such repetition of effect makes the penny drop and the reader becomes hyper-conscious of their recurring frequency. They begin to click by with the irritating regularity of telegraph poles seen from the window of a speeding train – those poles that speedily prevent us taking in the landscape beyond. Perhaps, the suspicion begins to dawn, this is what Chandler intended. When in doubt have two guys come through the door holding similes.

Hmmn ... similes like telegraph poles ... despite their pervasive presence throughout Chandler's work, this would appear, with proviso, an excellent juncture to minimise further reference to the figure of speech. The proviso is the quality of wit. The similes are packed with wit. And so is Marlowe. We like Marlowe and empathise with him in the same way that we like Falstaff. He makes us laugh – sometimes out loud. When the moment is right he can deliver a one-liner with the best of them. Famously, Marlowe was the recipient of 'a smile I could feel in my hip pocket.' When he is obliged to kill time in a restaurant bar he would never have entered of his own free will, Chandler sets him up to deliver a knock-out blow.

> A male cutie with henna'd hair drooped at a bungalow grand piano and tickled the keys lasciviously and sang 'Stairway to the Stars' in a voice with half the steps missing.

Making us laugh this mini-anecdote, although serving to underline Marlowe's disgruntledness, is essentially one of the one-on-one moments he allows us to share with him. But very frequently his sense of humour is put to pro-active dramatic use. When for instance in the course of *Farewell, My Lovely* Randall, one of Chandler's good cops quite correctly accuses Marlowe of having lied to him, the instant reply is:

> It was a pleasure.

Because we know that Marlowe had what he considered good and chivalrous reason to mislead Reynolds, we smile at this swift impertinence: we are pleased when the two men later become allies.

Chandler, then, chooses to invest Marlowe with a talent to amuse. In adding this dimension to his protagonist he is necessarily, then, if only in passing, slackening the pace of his storytelling to achieve, as he put it in that letter, an enhanced depth of focus. As well, making Marlowe the more engaging, he the more engages us.

But it is not merely the increased characterisation of its protagonist that gives the successor to *The Big Sleep* a more discursive narrative. A far greater influence on *Farewell, My Lovely*'s momentum than Marlowe *tout seul* is the manner in which the narrative turns outwards to concern itself with social and even political issues.

The Big Sleep's dynamic travels essentially in a straight line. There are, of course, sub-plots and cross-currents but basically, if crudely, it is the good guy against the bad guys in an arena that sits in the middle of a notional real world but in working, skulduggery practice remains insulated from everyday concerns. In *Farewell, My Lovely*, however, albeit at the level of the genre, the thriller action interfaces with institutions with which we, in our non private-eye lives, have some acquaintance. Specifically these are the areas of policing, politics and health care.

Raymond Chandler, it is well documented, had the same attitude to the governance of Santa Monica (aka Bay City) that Graham Greene had to the Mafioso-ridden Côte d'Azure. He had no doubt – he had been behind the scenes in the oil industry, remember – that there was something in the state of California that was very rotten indeed. Accordingly, in the playing out of one plot line in *Farewell, My Lovely* he paints us a picture of the Bay City Police Department that is corrupt and venal from top to bottom. The barrel is made up almost entirely of rotten apples. It is Marlowe's role, after sustaining great abuse, to come upon the scene and upset the apple barrel.

If this is to happen, however, Chandler must needs depict the barrel in all its sleazy complacency. This he does with great deftness showing us the mean, petty cruelties and illegalities of a bunch of crooked cops who carry out their daily abuses of privilege under the shadow of the gambling ships which sit like giant leeches just beyond the three mile limit. Such a process takes time in the unfolding on the page. Straight-line pace has to yield to a more leisurely taking on board of greater content. This does not mean the death of momentum. Indeed, because the content is absorbing (we start wondering about our own institutions!) there is arguably a build up of pressure that makes for, if less speed, greater momentum. Momentum in literature is of more account than pace.

The cops and mayor of Bay City are not only hand in glove with the flat-out hoods aboard the floating casinos – hand in till, rather – but also with another tranche of Bay City-based shysters. These are the illegally operating, essentially fake medicos.

(Southern) California has long had the unenviable reputation of being a natural home for crank religious sects, faddist health farms, inspirational psychotherapist movements. In *Farewell, My Lovely* Chandler offers up two practitioners of such dark pursuits for our delectation. The one is Dr Sonderborg, the other is Jules Amther – 'Psychic Consultant'.

Sonderborg runs a Bay City, well, 'sanatorium'. It is a private institution set up in the suitably converted interior of a large, private house in a pleasant residential area. Its least illegal activity is providing a drying out and aversion therapy haven for far-gone alcoholics. But given its barred windows and padded walls, all manner of other activities may so easily take place alongside this core resource. Illegal drugs may be trafficked. Men on the run may be given dubious sanctuary. Trouble makers – as witness Philip Marlowe – can be whipped off the streets (the Bay City police will provide transport and man power) and worked over chemically or with blunter instruments than a dirty hypodermic. If the treatment is excessive, the Pacific is conveniently to hand … It is the type of institution which can flourish in a country wedded to privatised medicine. Allegedly.

Since he practices a more esoteric scam the premises that Jules Amther operates from are harder to summarise. In essence they are those of a fortune-teller's crystal ball tent raised by a factor of a thousand to a level of sub-Bauhaus, modernist, minimalist bling. They reflect in steel and glass brick Amther's own appearance which is that of Bela Lugosi's good-looking brother.

> He was thin, tall and straight as a steel rod. He had the palest, finest white hair I ever saw. It could have been strained through silk gauze. His skin was as fresh as a rose petal. He might have been thirty-five or sixty-five. He was ageless. His hair was brushed straight back from as good a profile as Barrymore ever had.

On the strength of a description as fulsome as this we just know that Amther is going to prove just one total son-of-a-bitch charlatan. Marlowe has, indeed, already keyed in this conclusion, expressing his distaste for the man and defining his 'consultancy' not by describing its working practices but by allowing us to infer them from a contemptuous recital of Amther's food and drink clientele.

> Give him enough time and pay him enough money and he'll cure anything from a jaded husband to a grasshopper plague. He would be an expert in frustrated love affairs, women who slept alone and didn't like it, wandering boys and girls who didn't write home, sell the property now

or hold it for another year, will this part hurt me with my public or make me seem more versatile? Men would sneak in on him too, big strong guys that roared like lions around their offices and were all cold mush under their vests. But mostly it would be women, fat women that burned, old women that dreamed and young women that thought they might have Electra complexes, women of all sizes, shapes and ages. But with one thing in common – money. No Thursdays at the County Hospital for Mr Jules Amther. Cash on the line for him. Rich bitches who had to be dunned for their milk bills would pay him right now.

Ah yes. Southern California. Chandler, remember, had also worked in the accounts office of a dairy.

Chandler was writing *Farewell, My Lovely* as the 1930s neared their end. A decade earlier he had been well in the grip of chronic alcoholism and over the intervening years had experienced the extreme roller coaster highs and lows which the wagon that alcoholics climb on to and fall off travels. It has been suggested that in drawing these parallel portraits of Sonderborg and Amther, Chandler was drawing upon the in-depth research which, all unknowingly at the time, he had undertaken in his own past. Now, perhaps, aided by the larger-than-life licence of the thriller genre he was getting a few retaliatory licks in. It seems attractively plausible. But, then again, it is a premise which so many of us are predisposed to want to believe.

As the demands of Marlowe interacting with the world about him cause the plot line of *Farewell, My Lovely* to branch out, there is one sector of the underworld that emerges relatively unscathed – organised crime. All of Chandler's first three novels feature a night-spot-owning Mr Big with interests in maybe a dozen rackets and certainly controlling a swathe of corrupt policemen and city councillors. Yet all three of these unquestionable (sic) criminals go unpunished for their sins. Two of them are distinctly stylish in manner. (The third is less so: but he was formerly an actor ...) And the most stylish of all is Laird Brunette the Mr Big of *Farewell, My Lovely* – who, among other things, owns the gambling casinos moored off the Bay City coast line. Having trespassed aboard the one ship at extreme potential danger, Marlowe braces Brunette and the two box a taut, wary, respectful conversational draw. Marlowe has departed from Sonderborg saying contemptuously 'I leave you to dirtier hands than mine.' When, by contrast, favours having been negotiated and exchanged, he quits Brunette's office of his own free will, the two exchange a conventional but civilised 'good night' that comes after a freely-given hand shake.

Why should this be? On a low level of cunning there is always the commercial factor. There might just be a film rights deal. A smoothly attractive bad guy is always good box office. But I believe that over and above this a part of Chandler likes his Mr Bigs for the style with which he has endowed them. They speak and dress well. They have taste. And, above all, like Marlowe they have a species of honour. Honour among thieves may be a cliché but Brunette does live by a code. However else they may differ, Brunette and Marlowe, knight in sub-fusc armour, do have one thing in common. If either gives his word, that word will be honoured. Brunette on every level is utterly superior to the vulgarly venal John Wax, Bay City's Chief of Police.

As well as upon corrupt cops and shyster medicos Chandler

vents his spleen on a third human element in the Southern California mix – Joe Public. Wanting to get aboard one of the off-shore gambling ships Chandler is obliged to go down to the Bay City waterfront and lose himself among the just plain folks sampling the boardwalk delights. Initially he holes up in a cheap hotel.

> Cars honked along the alley they called the Speedway. Feet slithered on the sidewalks below my window. There was a murmur and a mutter of coming and going in the air. The air that seeped in through the rusted screens smelled of stale frying fat. Far off a voice of the kind that could be heard far off was shouting: 'Get hungry, folks. Get hungry. Nice hot doggies here. Get hungry ... '
> ... Outside, the narrow streets fumed, the sidewalks swarmed with fat stomachs. Across the street a bingo parlour was going full blast and beside it a couple of sailors with girls were coming out of a photographer's shop where they had probably been having their photographs taken riding on camels. The voice of the hot dog merchant split the dusk like an axe. A big blue bus blared down the street to the little circle where the street car used to turn on a turntable. I walked that way. After a while there was a faint smell of ocean. Not very much, but as if they had kept this much just to remind people this had once been a clean open beach where the waves came in and creamed and the wind blew and you could smell something besides hot fat and cold sweat.

On first reading this plaint might seem to point to a mordant vein of misanthropy in Chandler's make-up. And certainly other passages in other books, his frequently caustic correspondence, confirm that he entertained a savage indignation for the shoddy, the gimcrack and the turn-a-fast-buck meretricious. But it is clear in this passage that his ire is directed less at the would-be suckers and pleasure seekers than against the huckster enterprises selling the rubes short as, remorselessly trafficking in lowest common denominators, they never offer an even break. Chandler was shortly to purchase a home – that only one he ever owned – set on one of the most beautiful stretches of America's Pacific coast. Here he is lamenting the desecration of another such stretch in the opportunistic cause of commerce.

Chandler was not only prescient in flagging up the pimps and cowboys who would soon be flooding into Los Angeles alongside Dory Previn's Mary Cecilia Brown on the Malibu bus, he also gave clear-cut advance warning of the pre-packaged, fast-food, Disneyland culture that would convert the sons of the pioneers into prime-time addicted, Play Station-wielding, couch-potato obesities.

And in any case, earlier in *Farewell, My Lovely* he had already pre-empted any accusation of misanthropy. What meets Marlowe's investigating gaze when he visits Jessie Florian is unremittingly squalid. She has lived the most sordid of lives – crooked, promiscuous, lazy, self-centred. When, lying amid the grime and stink of her bedding she admits 'I feel like Death Valley', Marlowe (and Chandler) are brutal.

'And you look like a dead mule, I thought.'

But across the street it is a different story. Fronting Jessie Florian's place is the home of a Mrs Morrison, who after an absolutely conventional small-town life in the Iowan Midwest has found herself in old age and widowhood unaccountably (as it now seems) marooned in a run-down section of Los Angeles.

When Marlowe first quits the Florian pig-sty he catches sight of lace curtains opposite twitching and he dubs the watcher behind them 'Old Nosey'. We smile very faintly as we recognise the stock character. In due course Marlowe questions Mrs Morrison – she proves primly holier-than-thou – and then again with an LAPD Lieutenant. By now we have come to understand that spying on her neighbours is the only relief that Old Nosey can find to counter the intolerably crushing monotony of the desert in which in the final chapter of her life she has become lost. She gladly bears witness against Jessie Florian but, to savour the moment and her own importance, she embroiders and invents. The two professionals expertly and with casual ruthlessness cut this fake testimony back down to its proper size. Mortified, utterly distraught and bereft again now, she dissolves into tears. She flees from them sobbing uncontrollably. The men leave her house both hating themselves for having done what was necessary for them to do. It is a moment in which Chandler gives us not so much the still sad music of humanity as the tragic banality of pointless existence. It is a sequence written not so much by a misanthrope as by a fellow victim.

Like virtually all thrillers when laid out in cold blood on that Literary Morgue slab *Farewell, My Lovely* is revealed by forensic analysis as not being without dislocation in its structure. Although Chandler limns in a plausible route for her, the possibility that Little Velma could climb the ladder of success up and away from Central Avenue so far as to reach Aster Drive while leaving virtually no trace of the translation seems, on cool reflection, a lot less than likely. Nor, given her husband's super-rich compliance does it seem unduly necessary. That Marlowe should be used as a diversion-cum-decoy to conceal from Lindsay Marriott that that he is being lured to his death seems at one and the same time both over-engineered and simple-minded. The plotting here is a fossil from the original short-story 'Mandarin's Jade'. In the re-worked version there would have been far safer, far more direct, ways in which Mrs Grayle might have separated Marriott from both her own life and his. And if this new-upon-the-scene private eye incipiently digging into her past seemed to pose a threat, she would surely not have left him lying around in the land of the living.

Nevertheless, once again reflection of this sort is not what the reader of thrillers brings to the party. The foreground remains everything and, as Aristotle has already pointed out for us, if that foreground seems on first acquaintance to be credibly arrived at, the game is afoot.

Usually caused by that same tendency to over-reach which impairs the occasional simile, a few small blemishes arguably disfigure *Farewell, My Lovely*. One such is when Mrs Grayle puts her head back and goes into a peal of laughter causing Marlowe to tell us: 'I have only known four women in my life who could do that and still look beautiful.' Come on! The line is totally phony. The only response we can make to it has to be: 'Surely you mean five'. It is pretentiously sub-literary in a way that suggests Chandler had been reading Somerset Maugham.

And he directly engages with literature far too archly for my taste when in the final confrontation with Velma/Mrs Grayle he has Marlowe equate her victim, Marriott, with the Second Murderer in 'that scene in *King Richard III*'. It is a fact that at one time Chandler employed *The Second Murderer* as a working title for the book; it is true that the need to give Marlowe a cultural IQ making plausible the narrative tone of voice is an ongoing factor; but I inescapably feel that here Chandler breaks the thriller-melodrama mould for the cheap sake of wearing his own academic credentials on his sleeve. So, OK, he had pummelled the Shakespeare play at Dulwich or was re-reading it thirty-five years on. He had no need to highlight his familiarity with the text. His literary pedigree is implicit throughout his writing.

The High Window

WE HAVE SEEN THAT, ALTHOUGH IN the next breath he distinctly qualifies the judgment, in that 1949 letter to his Canadian admirer, Raymond Chandler cites *The High Window* as being the worst of the four novel-length thrillers he had written by that date. Perhaps further qualification is in order. After all, the book had not done badly by him. It was a reading of *The High Window* which prompted Charles Brackett, Billy Wilder's screenplay sparring partner to suggest that this unknown might be the writer to step into the gap his own disinclination to adapt *Double Indemnity* would create. That project was to render Chandler solvent and better for the first time in his life and, in due course, usher him into the forefront of public attention and the world of publishing's interest.

And certainly *The High Window* is neither the work of a journeyman apprentice or a manifestly dashed-off pot-boiler. Until, for instance, the irreverence of Marlowe's persona is made intentionally to intrude, the carefully crafted opening paragraphs describing the 'big solid cool-looking' Murdoch house in select Pasadena might serve as the beginning of hundreds of overtly more 'serious' – but ultimately inferior – novels of the last hundred years. They bear comparison with the brief, bravura description Fitzgerald offers of the West Egg landscaping running up to the door-step of the Buchanan residence with that *élan* only the super-rich can commandeer from assisted nature. Landscapes and cityscapes, street-scenes and buildings are settings and backdrops and set pieces that Chandler always does with graceful aplomb. He has that keenness of sight which allows him to select the most telling features; and the linguistic and syntactical grace to effect a translation on to the page which allows us to share his vision.

It is easy, while on the subject, to pay such lip-service to the quality of Chandler's writing line by line as I have just passingly done. It is time, perhaps, to offer a single token for the so many other deeds accomplished elsewhere. Early in the narrative Marlowe needs to visit the Los Angeles district that was once its nineteenth-century centre.

> Bunker Hill is old town, lost town, crook town. Once, very long ago, it was the choice residential district of the city, and there are still standing a few of the jigsaw Gothic mansions with wide porches and walls covered with round-end shingles and full corner bay windows with spindle turrets. They are all rooming houses now, their parquetry floors are scratched and worn through the once glossy finish and the wide sweeping staircases are dark with time and with cheap varnish laid on over generations of dirt. In the tall rooms haggard landladies bicker with shifty tenants. On the wide cool front porches, reaching

their cracked shoes into the sun and staring at nothing sit the old men with faces like lost battles ...

Out of the apartment houses come women who should be young but have faces like stale beer; men with pulled-down hats and quick eyes that look the street over behind the cupped hand that shields the match flame; worn intellectuals with cigarette coughs and no money in the bank; fly cops with granite faces and unwavering eyes; cokies and coke peddlers; people who look like nothing in particular and know it, and once in a while even men that actually go to work. But they come out early, when the wide cracked side-walks are empty and still have dew on them.

It may be argued that since a tramp is easier to describe than a suburban bank manager this is an easy target to hit. But nevertheless, needing to introduce a crime and punishment ambiance of menace for his thriller purposes, Chandler scores an absolute bull's-eye. There are those details. The shingles have round-ends. The shoes are not only cracked they are being stretched forward to meet the warmth of the sun. They are worn by owners whom Chandler, inverting conventional structure the better to maximise impact, refrains from introducing as his subject until the end of the sentence. The cheap varnish has been lazily superimposed not merely over the *in situ* dust but also over 'generations of dirt'. How telling is that humanising, yet de-humanising specification. There is the careful but unobtrusive variation between long and short sentences. There are the interior cadences. In the tall rooms haggard landladies do not come and go talking of Michaelangelo (as for a nano-second we thought they might) what superior adjective might improve on 'haggard' or its deducible associate words 'bicker' and 'shifty'? Finally, there are the hallmark similes. In this excerpt they are pushed to the functional limit and not an inch beyond.

Bunker Hill – where Marlowe is about to find a newly-minted corpse – is sad and grungy and bereft. And how beautifully this is emphasised by the concluding indication that once and somewhere else there was or is another kind of life. Allowing for local variations, Chandler achieves narrative effects such as this throughout his novels. The negative consequence of this is that if we do not take care we may come to take the quality of his prose for granted. We should take care not to.

But even when in the right order fine words do not of themselves a thriller make any more than do picturesque descriptions. It would seem that, looking beyond the immediate surface, we should return to considering what grounds Chandler believed he had for disparaging his third full-length book. What I think such a considering suggests is that Chandler's reasons for being dissatisfied fall into two distinct categories. Thoroughly absorbing though it is, I believe we should not allow the one any lasting influence upon our appraisal of *The High Window* as a book being judged on the basis of what appears between its covers. Chandler did not, it seems evident, obey this fundamental rule of literary criticism. He was guilty of overlaying upon his own assessment of this particular work the uncomfortable memories of the grind, the emotional blood, sweat and tears its long genesis cost him.

Even in his early short-story pulp days when money was tight and every word that made it into print brought in a few cents more, Chandler was never prolific. His self-imposed need to refine, polish, find the *mot juste*, the most functional rhythm ensured that he would always be light-years away from the output of an Erle Stanley Gardner or a Simenon. *The High Window* took two years in the writing and, while this was a shorter period than Flaubert would have required, it still came as the third in a straight, uninterrupted succession of three novel-length works. For Chandler this added up to a Marathon stint and as he toiled with this last he was beginning to hit the wall. He was tired as he wrote and tiring further. And this increasing fatigue would have stemmed from more than the general sense of being on a treadmill.

As touched on above, it is a truism that for every writer of fiction the highest hurdle to surmount is the second book. Perhaps everybody does have 'that one book in them'. Certainly examples are legion of promising, even excellent, first novels that never knew a successor and whose authors' names are long since forgotten. This observation is relevant here because *The High Window*, Chandler's third book, was in working practice, virtually his second. *Farewell, My Lovely* is literally the second, of course, but since its plot-lines are based on the combining of those two pulp stories, its armature came to Chandler largely pre-fabricated. Given this, the fleshing out, the layering in of detail and nuance and inference, would have appeared almost monumentally less daunting.

The High Window, by contrast, is built upon a wholly original plot newly spun out of Chandler's wits and immediate devising. Plotting is difficult. It is difficult in all fiction but particularly so in thrillers where it is the be-all and end-all. Chandler by his own frequent admission was poor when it came to plotting. Rather than the totally worked through flow-chart of a plot mapped out on graph paper, as it were, he tended to improvise his way along allowing the local and immediate inspiration of the foreground scene or sequence to act as a signpost generally indicating the direction of another enticing set-piece further downstream. The danger here, clearly, is of venturing too far and for too long down blind alleys, of writing oneself into a corner and thus to find perhaps weeks of hard-won and in itself good writing quite superfluously beside the point. Reaching these impasses, it was not in Chandler's nature to cut and paste. He would return to 'Go' and begin again. To work forward with the eventuality of this worst-case scenario occurring never quite laid to rest must have been – it is! – extremely stressful. I have no doubt that in its doing *The High Window* stressed Chandler a very depressing great deal.

In overview terms there are two aspects of a thriller or whodunnit which, from day one, will tax the author close to nervous breakdown and remain at his shoulder until long after he or she has finished the writing. The first is the matter of concealing the identity of the core villain. For the author, seeing the whole picture in a sense in the first quickening instant of conception, that identity will be as conspicuously obvious as … well, a tarantula on a slice of angel food.

The second (and linked) anxiety that will plague an author from the word go to the finishing line is an ever-nagging doubt as to the plausibility, the effectiveness, of the story's 'MacGuffin' – that nexus of cause and effect, logic, motivational stimulus, coincidence and gimmick that gets the premise upon which the story-line is based off and running and keeps it ongoingly credible as the complications, the thrills and spills ensue. (In *Casablanca* the MacGuffin is the letters of transit – ridiculous when you think about it. Major Strasser could just have burned or chosen to ignore them.) In the case of *The High Window* Chandler must have been the victim of sharply nagging doubts on one of these fronts.

He had small cause to worry over the matter of keeping the identity of his core villain concealed. It is not at all obvious who this may be and, in any case, the attribution of guilt and responsibility as the story concludes is intentionally somewhat blurred. With a quixotic exercise of his own sense of what is fitting – a judgment we feel to be justified – Marlowe refrains from turning no less than two murderers in to face due process of Law, opting instead to let them stew in their own guilt-ridden juices. All of this passes muster.

But the quality of *The High Window*'s cause and effect plotting must have given Chandler many sleepless nights. It is simplistically poor in the extreme.

As so often in Chandler, blackmail lies close to the centre of things. But in this deployment the 'goods' that the blackmailer has on the victim do not begin to cut the mustard. Against all credible odds (but very much to the convenience of the author) the blackmailer had a camera in his hands which was pointing in the right direction (and with the correct shutter speed and focal length set) when, way above where he would have been naturally looking, the victim of a murderous shove from behind found the window he was looking out from to be very high indeed. This simply isn't on. But neither is the final outcome of this totally stretched happenstance when Marlowe finds the resulting incriminating photograph and negative by, in virtual effect, stumbling over them. They have been concealed in a hiding place tricksy in terms of the immediate needs of fiction but where no grown-up blackmailer would have for a single, solitary moment risked leaving them.

This is a huge and inherent and, yes, nagging weakness at the heart of *The High Window* and Chandler was plainly utterly aware that it was such. He opts – desperately – for double bluff. When, beginning to explain to Merle Davis, the plot's hugely put-upon fall-girl, that she is innocent of any crime, Marlowe shows her the photograph which incriminates somebody else and says:

> I found it last night, by a fluke of the same sort that was involved in the taking of the picture. Which is a fair sort of justice.

Yeah, Ray. Sure. But grade-school plotting.

There is one 'stretcher', however, that Chandler does succeed in most adroitly smuggling past our disbelief. This is the convincing us that a young girl, witness but nothing else more, to the murder of a man who once sexually molested her, could be thoroughly persuaded that she herself was the perpetrator of the crime. To pull off this trick Chandler reaches for his Freud – just possibly, let us not forget, in the original German.

At this period (hard on the heels of his death) Freud's theories were beginning to percolate down to what we might in shorthand terms call Admass culture and receive modish, passing, not to mention credit-seeking, show-off mention in contemporary novels and films. (*Kings Row, Undercover, Leave Her to Heaven* furnish film examples). Chandler, once again ahead of rather than following a trend does rather better than the fleetingly modish.

Furnishing Marlowe with an outstandingly civilised, cool and intelligent personal physician, Carl Moss – 'a big burly Jew', be it noted – Chandler has this expert witness account to him and so to us how Merle Davis has been able to persist in this misplaced belief that she herself was responsible for the murder to which she was an eyewitness.

'Does she think he jumped out of the window on her account?' the doctor sensibly asks Marlowe. The following exchange then follows:

> 'I don't know. Mrs Murdock is the man's widow. She married again and her second husband is dead too. Merle has stayed with her. The old woman treats her like a rough parent treats a naughty child.'
>
> 'I see. Regressive.'
>
> 'What's that?'
>
> 'Emotional shock and the subconscious attempt to escape back to childhood. If Mrs Murdock scolds her a good deal, but not too much, that would increase the tendency. Identification of childhood subordination with childhood protection.'
>
> 'Do we have to go into that stuff?' I growled. He looked at me calmly.
>
> 'Look, pal. The girl's obviously a neurotic. It's partly induced and partly deliberate. I mean to say that she really enjoys a lot of it. Even if she doesn't realise that she enjoys it.'

And so on. To anyone versed in matters psychiatric this may appear as no more than so much flim-flam. But in the context of a book already possessed with its depiction of a dominating mother and her son of a distinct Oedipal undertow, this is flim-flam that convinces me a whole sight better than a plot-convenient rationalisation that two inordinate flukes butted up back to back cancel each other out.

The liberation of Merle Davis from her eight years of durance vile in the psychiatric dungeon Mrs Murdock has contrived for her provides the upbeat ending to *The High Window* and endorses the authoritatively definitive Dr Carl Moss's statement to Marlowe that he is a 'shop-soiled Galahad'. I find this plot-line more compelling than the ducking and diving of the novel's parallel narrative thrust – the attempt to pull off a major forgery coup. Since he had become type-cast as a thriller writer and was contractually obligated to a publisher it was never going to happen, but I find myself wondering now if Chandler might not have been better advised to treat the Merle Davis story head-on as a straight psychological melodrama and this time around leaving an unemployed Marlowe cooling his heels on his office desk.

The travails generated by the writing of *The High Window* caused another epistolary wail to fly speeding through the US Mail. In a 1942 letter to Blanche Knopf Chandler predicted: 'I'm afraid the book is not going to be any good to you. No action, no likeable characters, no nothing. The detective does nothing.'

Brave words to forward to the decision-making wife of your publisher; desperate ones from a writer in mid-stream. But they constitute, we might feel, an instance of protesting too much.

It is true that this is the least thrilling Chandler thriller – the one in which Marlowe is asked to be most passive. In its course he isn't sapped unconscious, drugged, worked over by the police or in any more general way placed in jeopardy. He goes about the business of unravelling the two coincidentally linked blackmail and forgery plots largely unthreatened. *The High Window* thus comes nearest of all Chandler's books to resembling that English-style whodunit of the Dorothy Sayers type which – rightly, I myself feel – he chose to disparage in his essay 'The Gentle Art of Murder'. Without too many adjustments Lord Peter Wimsey – and certainly a resurrected Walter Gage – could have navigated themselves through the self-same landscape.

That said, although structurally the same, such a hypothetical work might have been inert – possibly to the point of unreadability. It would have lacked the world-weary humour, the wisecracks and the similes. It would have lacked that impression of integrity which Marlowe imparts as he passages through territories peopled almost entirely by morally dubious and scuzzy characters. It would probably have been devoid of any vein of what we can call social commentary. There is not a great deal of such comment in *The High Window* as against *Farewell, My Lovely* – the police, for example, are nothing like so pro-actively criminal but merely stupid and lazily inept. But in one instance Chandler is again ahead of the pack and curve in identifying a malignant forerunner of the shape of US things to come. His inquiries take Marlowe into a selectedly privileged – but not distinguished – gated community. Beyond the barriers a five-star night-club with ten-star rip-off capability is to be found and about the surrounding sunlit valleys and broad uplands lie scattered the bling-filled residences of the super-rich. This is Idle Valley (Sic). Security provision here is provided by The Idle Valley Patrol which is dedicated to keeping what's theirs theirs. That is to say Idle Valley enjoys possession of its own private, crypto-fascist police force complacently, since money talks, operating outside of Federal and State laws. Well before the War of '42

Chandler is offering us an early glimpse of the armed camp, gated communities that, like melanomas, have increasingly pockmarked the desirable residential landscape of America.

In Marlowe's *Farewell, My Lovely* office a calendar hangs on the wall.

> They had Rembrandt on the calendar that year ... It showed him holding a smeared palette with a dirty thumb and wearing a tam o'shanter which wasn't too clean either. His other hand held a brush poised in the air, as if he might be going to do a little work after a while, if somebody made a down payment. His face was ageing, saggy, full of the disgust of life and the thickening effects of liquor. But it had a cheerfulness that I liked, and the eyes were as bright as drops of dew.

After several re-readings of *The High Window* a question starts to insinuate. Why Rembrandt? Why not the Golden Gate Bridge, Old Faithful, Joe Di Maggio, Rita Hayworth? The answer may reside, I think, in the truth that if the 1940 LAPD had been required to pull in all the middle-aged men in town answering to this description, men, that is, with disgust and 'the thickening effects of liquour' in their face, one of the first to appear in the line-up would have been Raymond Thornton Chandler.

I do not for a moment suggest that Chandler was so monumentally foolish or vainglorious as to equate himself and his work with Rembrandt and his. But he did, I think, hold up Rembrandt to himself as that type of indomitable genius whose example a lesser man – one Life has afflicted with the same insults – could do no better than try to emulate, however distantly. Chandler knew that by the time he executed this portrait,

Rembrandt, so often his own worst enemy, had indeed been well and truly beaten up by Life in terms of all material things. We know this too. But in recalling the vicissitudes visited upon him we tend not to dwell on booze. An alcoholic would. Chandler, in tipping his hat to the far greater artist was, I believe, saluting him for his endurance, his persistence: that dedicated returning to his last time after calamity and poverty stricken time. In describing this calendar – identical, surely, to one on his own wall – Chandler is trying to pledge to himself to hang on in there and to keep coming up with his own best shot. Despite the drink. For there is in the description too the shadow cast by the fear that he himself might turn out to be one who might not be going to do a little work either after a while or ever again. If the Paramount-Billy Wilder anecdotage dating from 1943 is to be taken as gospel, at the time of writing *The High Window* Chandler must have been once more battling with his drink problem.

The book contains interior evidence. In the course of the formal police investigation into the murder that has taken place on Bunker Hill, Detective-Lieutenant Jesse Breeze and his assistant, Spangler, brace Marlowe in his own apartment. Breeze, tough, cynical, world-weary but, we come to learn, essentially honourable has already studiously avoided taking a drink higher up the narrative. Now, however, host in his own home, Marlowe fixes some highballs. This is what ensues:

> [I] set the tray down on the cocktail table in front of the davenport where Breeze was sitting. I took two of the glasses, handed one to Spangler, and took the other to my chair.
>
> Spangler held the glass uncertainly, pinching his lower

lip between thumb and finger, looking at Breeze to see whether he would accept the drink.

Breeze looked at me very steadily. Then he sighed. Then he picked the glass up and tasted it and sighed again and shook his head sideways with a half smile; the way a man does when you give him a drink and he needs it very badly and it is just right and the first swallow is a peek into a cleaner, sunnier, brighter world.

For those with eyes to see it, this beautifully orchestrated little incident is the depiction – is there a better one written anywhere else? – of a man falling headlong off the wagon into a world that is not going to remain sunny, bright and clean for very much longer. The evocation of 'the first swallow' has all the exactitude of experience. This is Chandler in oblique confessional mode and I believe it conveys every indication that while he was writing *The High Window* he was fighting a bitter on-off, win-some, lose-some, battle with his drinking problem. We can surmise that spiritually there is no harder period in an alcoholic's downward spiralling.

If Chandler was to nurture bad feelings about *The High Window* in years to come, it was not only, I suggest, because he was obliged to progress it keenly aware of its cornball, unconvincing central plot premise, or because Marlowe was in quiescent mode, or because he had constantly to rack his brains to construct a twisting and turning plot from scratch. Perhaps the prime reason for *The High Window* delivering long-term bad vibrations was because he was unable to forget that every time he sat down at his desk his nerves, precisely as the nerves of the failed writer he was to depict in a short story a decade later, Hank Bruton, were jangling from an excess or insufficiency of liquor.

The Lady in the Lake

WE MIGHT IMAGINE THAT AFTER TWO years or more of toiling away at the resistance into which *The High Window* had hardened, Chandler, on at long last completing it, would have taken a leaf out of his protagonist's book and, tilting back in his chair, put his feet up on the desk the better to savour the pleasures of unemployment. Such was not the case. Needs must when the rent book drives. Even if in his own stop-go, stop-begin-again manner he had completed three novels as well as better than half a dozen financially necessary short stories since Alfred Knopf had first invited a full-length 'pulp' in 1938, there could be no stepping down from the treadmill. Selling modestly, this body of work had failed to set the Hudson very much on fire. Granting himself little or no respite Chandler turned to a fourth novel-length thriller. Or rather, to put this period of grindstone pressure into more accurate perspective, he turned *back* and once again revisited previous material.

One of the factors contributing to Chandler's creative unease in the late 30s, early 40s, must surely have been that with several projects often on the stocks simultaneously he would find himself trying to work both sides of the mean street at once. A memorandum he subsequently drew up for the tax authorities as he pursued a tax claim makes this clear. But his own mind would have been less than clear at the time. At any moment he was working on one story the grass would have been growing daily greener on several others. Distraction does not make for full speed ahead.

But among the slew of work he had finished was his 1939 short story, 'The Lady in the Lake'. This was what could now serve to provide him with a foot on the ground basis for a fourth novel. Reverting to his former practice he fused elements from this with matter drawn from two other of his 'pulps' – 'Bay City Blues' (1938) and 'No Crime in the Mountains' (1941). This recycling technique must have brought some reassurance. After the water torture trials of spinning the matter of *The High Window* out from his own invention, he once again had the use of a pre-existing road map.

This no doubt accounts for the fact that although it oscillates between two different topographical centres, Bay City and Puma Lake (aka Santa Monica and Big Bear Lake), on first reading – the one, to repeat, that counts – *The Lady in the Lake* impresses as a tightly-plotted thriller sustaining an on-going momentum. It demonstrates all of those attributes that Chandler in one of his low moments bemoaned were missing from *The High Window*. Marlowe is pro-active; he does encounter direst personal jeopardy and assaults; there are (a handful of) nice characters. Moreover, although it is never, of course, the main event in a Chandler book, a satisfying element of whodunnit mystery underlies the narrative's foreground action. The machinations of the bad guys are devious and it is not quite obvious for a considerable while who has done just what to whom.

The armature, then, of *The Lady in the Lake* is perfectly serviceable and this seems to have aided Chandler in maintaining his high standards in local, line by line, paragraph by paragraph, effects. The excellence and appropriateness of the similes I think we can by now take as read: so too the confrontational cracking wise. The gimlet-eyed descriptions are as telling as ever – and there is a pleasant extension to their subject matter.

Of all the many locations in and around Los Angeles that Raymond and Cissy Chandler transiently occupied during the many years before their finally coming to rest in La Jolla, his own favourite was their cabin in the San Bernardino Mountains. (It seems to have been only mountain winters and the need imposed by Cissy's deteriorating condition for close to hand health care amenities that drew them back to LA.) In setting much of *The Lady in the Lake* action around, in effect, Big Bear Lake, Chandler needed to extend beyond his mean-street, tract-housing, Malibu-bling descriptions. Succinctly he rises to the occasion splendidly. The impressions he gives us of the high-altitude landscape, its flora, its bird life, its (overtly) tranquil cleanliness are beautifully observed, and if not set down in the exact same rhythms of a W.H. Hudson or H.E. Bates no less evocative.

> I turned the Chrysler into this and crawled carefully around huge bare granite rocks and past a little waterfall and through a maze of black oak trees and ironwood and manzanita and silence. A blue jay squawked on a branch

and a squirrel scolded at me and beat one paw angrily on the pine cone it was holding. A scarlet-topped woodpecker stopped probing in the bark long enough to look at me with one beady eye and then dodge behind the tree trunk to look at me with the other one.

Eyeball to eyeball it seems the squirrel got as good as it gave. Because, in Chandler's case, it had been, the country surrounding Puma Lake comes across as authentically 'lived in'.

Since in putting much of his old wine into this new novel-length bottle Chandler was returning to Bay City, there is a return as well in *The Lady in the Lake* to what I have loosely labelled 'social comment'. Once again we meet a shifty, malpractising doctor, shooting too readily from the hip with his bent hypodermics. Once more – at one time Chandler was going to give *The Lady in the Lake* the title *Law is Where You Buy It* – we encounter a range of dubious cops. There are brain-dead uniforms, devoid of original thought. There are middle-ranking opportunists whose any thoughts of protecting and serving have long since been eroded by the system and their certain knowledge that their personal best interests will be served through playing it by the Captain's book and not the Law. And, in particular there is one cop, a major character, who is a genuinely disturbing blend of savagery, single-mindedness and motivated malignancy – a malignancy the more menacing for being closer to intelligence than to stupidity. We also, to be sure, come across good cops in *The Lady in the Lake* and with Marlowe's catalytic help by the novel's end they are left – briefly, we cannot but feel – possessors of the local field. One such is the Chief of the Bay City Police Department. The other is Puma Lake's Constable and Deputy

Sheriff John Patton, a character whom, in due course, we must examine in his role as *The Lady in the Lake*'s second hero.

Once again Joe Public, the 'great unwashed' public, gaudy, vulgar, loud, crude appetite-driven Admass of the Bay City boardwalk, are on the receiving end of Chandler's scorn. Now, in high summer, they have migrated up to the cooler temperatures of the mountains for their vacational break and their shirts and voices louder, their comments and behaviour cruder, their trashiness trashier, they earn the contempt of the local residents long into the nights. There is, in fact, in *The Lady in the Lake* a (barely) latent reminder that 'God made the Country, but Man made the Town.' Chandler has long since been honoured as the prose poet of Los Angeles but in *The Lady in the Lake* he clearly offers the opinion that it is in the city that you may find the biggest hogs in the biggest troughs.

Something else is close to latent in *The Lady in the Lake*: World War II.

It is relevant, I believe, to recall at this juncture that after the outbreak of war in Europe in late 1939 Chandler attempted to repeat what he had done over two decades earlier and enlist in a Canadian regiment. Unlike the six-years-younger Dashiell Hammett who had opted to enlist in the US Army, Chandler, at fifty-one, was rejected immediately on grounds of age. (Hammett, was inducted, served his country with unobtrusive heroism doing tours of duty in the Aleutians. On his discharge he returned to find that country fit only to egregiously betray him.) It might just have been imagined, therefore, that chagrined by this rejection Chandler in over-compensating mood might have sought to do his fighting on the page by penning a not so oblique blood and guts saga that would stiffen the sinews of every red-blooded American boy and send him on his way to give Hirohito's little buck-toothed bandits their comeuppance. This was not the case. Having gone to the wars Chandler knew what it was like. He shadows the off-stage presence of World War II into *The Lady in the Lake* in passing in the most delicate manner.

Such delicacy, however, is conspicuously absent from the late short story 'No Crime in the Mountains' (1941) that made up a significant portion of the full-length thriller's template. Set in the same San Bernardino mountains it is one of Chandler's worst efforts. He offers us a Marlowe surrogate tangling with enemy aliens intent on undermining the US economy by flooding the country with fake bank notes. The characters – a Hun and a Jap! – are made of pure Central Casting cardboard. There is an interesting local law enforcement officer in the tale but I believe its prime virtue may have been that writing it may have brought home to Chandler the existence of a generic problem.

The outbreak of the War of '39 (as Europeans are apt to think of it) put the pulp magazine industry and Hollywood into an awkward no-man's-land. 'Over there' one hell of a spectacular shoot-'em-up had broken out. On the land, in the air, on the sea it was death or glory all the way. There was just one drawback. All this boffo box-office violence was a strictly un-American activity. You couldn't show Cooper or Gable fully-frontally holding off the Panzers outside of Dunkirk.

Hollywood's fall-back answer to this little location difficulty was the same as Chandler's with 'No Crime in the Mountains': to bring the war back across the Atlantic and fight it on the home front in the only way possible. A series of espionage thrillers – *All*

Through the Night, Across the Pacific, Saboteur, others – were made. They may contain incidental virtues but, in essence, none of them work. Their common defect is that they all have essentially what are gangster or caper plots unconvincingly made over to suit the phoney war times. Instead of the suave Mr Big with a casino just over the county line or the gutter rat Chicago mobster making his move on the South Side, we find the suave diplomat attached to the legation or the Japanese 'sleeper' long since planted States-side. And since little authentic anecdote about such real life activities was to hand, since Hollywood had established no genre convention for such subject matter and the pulps no snappy, convincing shorthand, these attempts at indigenous spy thrillers largely fail to convince.

I suspect that by the time he had finished 'No Crime in the Mountains' Chandler had perceived that there was more impact, more final truth to be derived from the morality play deployment of a stylised crime melodrama with its scope for suggestion than from the head-on but superficial huffing and puffing of a quasi-authentic 'documentary'.

Although World War II had well and truly landed on America's doorstep well before the completion of *The Lady in the Lake*, the book's narrative line is entirely driven by standard issue home elements. The crimes Marlowe messes with are domestic and civilian. Only the faintest incidental references that two minor characters – a gigolo, a routinely less than straight cop – are waiting to be inducted and a forward-looking reference to the fact that the lights on the Malibu coast line will soon be blacked out (the book's action takes place before Pearl Harbor: it was completed after) inform us that beyond the immediate proceedings the war is being progressed off-stage. And so, barely, sub-textually, almost, for those who wish to discern it, Chandler introduces into the work a strain he has not given us before. On the edge of conscious thought we sense that with something so immense taking place outside these pages what happens within them, for all its local shocks and violence is precisely that: local. It may not add up to much more than the hill of beans. And yet, it is here. Somebody should do something about it.

On what evidence he draws in saying so (he cites no letter or other source) Tom Hiney, Chandler's 1997 biographer, declares that *The Lady in the Lake* was the only novel Chandler wrote that he could never bring himself to reread in later years. Having said of *The High Window* that it lacked 'verve' Hiney now says of its successor that it shows Marlowe at his most misanthropic and, worse, since staring into a mirror Marlowe tells us:

> I brushed my hair and looked at the grey in it. There was getting to be plenty of grey in it. The face under the hair had a sick look. I didn't like the face at all.

We now have to contemplate a Marlowe who is growing old and, as Hiney puts it, 'certainly does not feel like a hero any more.'

Well now ... It had never occurred to me until reading this – and it still does not – that Marlowe was ever intended to register as a Superman hero. He may be a latter-day knight-errant, true, but he is also Everyman – our own best selves as we would like to think. Each time he goes down a mean street, he has to steel himself. Everymen are human. They age. Chandler would have had no truck with annually re-cloning a two-dimensional, eyes-and-teeth, brand-name-dropping clothes horse like James Bond and serving him up on another cardboard plate with a slick of verve sauce.

Around 1942, rejected by the military for being just that, old, Chandler would have been tired and feeling it. He would have been intensely saddened, distraught even, by the daily news from Europe where the Nazis, having desecrated the Germany he had once so taken to, had now stormtrooped their way to the Channel. Yes, there was a lot going on in the world now for a man in his mid-fifties to feel old and tired about. And misanthropic too. If this were you and you were a writer of fiction you might well endow your chief protagonist with some of these very attributes. You would confront him with those who might provide him with good and proper reason to wax misanthropic. You would ask of captious critics: do you really believe that 'verve' is the be-all and end-all of a thriller that sets out to be worth reading more than once?

Hiney also observes:

> The corpses neither surprise nor shock Marlowe any more. The sight of death simply seems to confirm his dejected attitude: 'I sat very still,' he says on finding one body in a shower, 'and listened to the evening grow quiet outside the windows. And very slowly I grew quiet with it.'

Well, now ... Hiney's account is, in fact, grossly misleading. Marlowe does not, if you return to the text, find a body and then dejectedly award himself a solitary time out. Had he done so he might well, I concede, have been reacting in a somewhat nerveless manner. But, in fact, the sequence of events in a somewhat bad day out of his office is rather more action packed. Namely, attempting to further question a dubious witness he is abruptly confronted by a thoroughly flakey woman who advances on him holding a gun. For some terrible seconds Marlowe is convinced she will shoot him. Instead, just as abruptly, she gives him the gun and leaves. The gun is empty but has just been fired. Marlowe finds some of the bullets in a body which is indeed in a shower. He now drives to touch base with his client (whose interests he is obliged to protect) and with a woman who may be implicated in the shower killing. He then returns to the scene of the crime and calls the police. When they arrive, the police variously insult and humiliate Marlowe, one of them slapping him around – an insult which, biting his lip, he tolerates. Finally, in the evening, he is released by the police and returns to his office. It is there that he winds down and slowly grows quiet along with the evening.

This is not the behaviour either of a dejected or callously uncaring man. Marlowe has spent the day being as busy as the one-legged man in a forest fire and his response when he is at last left to his own devices is both civilised and grown up. We can sense he has been shocked by the gruesome death. We realise that he has the need to lower his adrenalin count and collect his thoughts and regain his balance. This has been a day on which he has, as yet unknowingly, crossed the path of two murderers and his method for coming to this knowledge will not be fuelled by verve but by intelligent, occasionally two-fisted, and, yes, maybe a touch tired, persistence.

Not every character Marlowe comes across in *The Lady in the Lake* is a fitting target for either his misanthropy or ours. There are a few class act personages entirely deserving of our respect. This leads towards another sub-textual element in the book which

I am almost loath to draw attention to, it is so vestigial, so little more than a shadow of a hint. Nevertheless ...

I have asserted that the Sternwood mansion in *The Big Sleep* cannot begin to do duty as the Great Good Place. It is just conceivable that Puma Lake, out of season be it understood, may be intended to embody a latter-day Eden. Certainly it has been contaminated by city values but something at its heart still remains pristine. There is something at Puma Lake capable of acting as a compass bearing for anyone seeking to shake the venal dust of the city and its ways off their shoes. Puma Lake just might constitute the site of a good deed in our shabby, war-wearied lives. It is true that no angels seem to hover above its honky-tonkish main drag but it is just possible that we could find God there. God in this manifestation is Town Constable John Patton.

Patton, in more ways than one, is the best 'good' character that Chandler put down on paper. Interestingly, he is forever addressing Marlowe as 'son'. Referring to himself as 'old' (at an age I remember regarding long ago as the prime of life), Patton is given the same age that Chandler had reached when he described him but in all other respects the two are chalk and cheese. Chandler was urbane and cosmopolitan. The fictional Patton is a good old, a country boy. Chandler was beginning to be broken down by age and (possibly) sex. Patton, big, overweight, can go on all day. The excess pounds are still, somehow solid and make him a bear of a man, a man solid as a rock. But not between the ears. Chandler could read Euripides, Marlowe plays a fair game of chess: but arguably, with or without verve, it is Patton who has the mind that comes closest to outperforming a steel trap. And Patton, despite his outwardly cracker-barrelled manner, is ultimately a gentleman to his finger-tips. When, still suspiciously uncertain about this LA private eye and his motives, he invites Marlowe to join him and Mrs Patton for dinner in his home, we glimpse a crucial microcosm of what a bright and civilised world this could be without the hoodlums and the wars.

The very name – Patton – is intriguing. Are we to suppose that, prescient yet again, Chandler was tipping his hat to the US general he was predisposed to put most faith in. I suppose not ... John Patton's weapon of choice is a vast Colt revolver. He only has the one whereas George S. Patton had two and pear-handled at that. But when push comes to fast draw at the conclusion of *The Lady in the Lake* John Patton's use of his chosen weapon leaves us in no doubt that getting there firstest with his mostest, he could shoot five-star rings around – or off – his namesake. Growing to respect each other as professionals, as men, Marlowe and Patton come in effect to double team. They need to. Their ultimate adversary as *The Lady in the Lake* comes to its confrontational conclusion is as intimidating a bill of goods as Chandler ever drew up.

In 'Bay City Blues', one of the pulp prototypes for *The Lady in the Lake*, Chandler came the closest he ever came to a Jim Thomsonesque hero-villain when he depicted plainclothes copper Lieutenant Al De Spain. De Spain is a piece of work. Big, hard, sadistic, he is capable both physically and mentally, as he proves, in beating out of a professional strong-arm hoodlum confession to a crime he has not committed. Because authentic seeming, the scene, watched in obligatory, non-intervening silence by the Marlowe surrogate, is the most sickeningly brutal Chandler ever gave us. In *The Lady in the Lake*'s fuller lengthed re-working of the De Spain plot-line, the same force for evil reappears, his name now extended to Degarmo.

Probably elevating his sights above the pulp constituency, Chandler dilutes and tamps down the sheer brutality quotient for his longer version but Degarmo, hard as nails, conscienceless, corrupt, respecter of no rules, intelligent and totally embedded among other killers in the neighbourhood, is a murderous opponent to play tag with in Bay City. Or, indeed, in Puma Lake.

A little ahead of us, as on a first reading I fancy Chandler usually makes his detective, Marlowe entices Degarmo up to Puma Lake ostensibly to stick a murder rap on his original client. Marlowe's real object is to get Degarmo in Patton's back yard where the odds of survival will be better. It is as well he does this. Degarmo, his eye on securing the fall guy he needs, is diverted enough to lower his guard and it is enough for Patton to thwart him – but not kill. Although presented with a chance to shoot Degarmo in the back in rapidly cooling blood, Patton stays his hand and, doing so, preserves one foothold at least for himself untainted in the Puma Lake Eden.

Marlowe's contribution to this complex finale has been knowingly to spend long, long hours one-on-one with a man he has deduced is a violent, ruthless and highly efficient killer. In executing this role he may not have displayed much verve: but his nerve has been total and the thriller's tension commensurate.

Four separate murders have criss-crossed by the conclusion of *The Lady in the Lake* and the plot, by and large, seems intriguing in its complexity, ongoing in its development, plausibly logical as to cause and effect. And yet ... forensic analysis upon the literary morgue slab soon brings about very apparent deconstruction.

The basic premise, to begin with, the factor which links Bay City and Puma Lake, requires a huge geographical coincidence. A key character has to be common to both. But such happenstances do happen in life and with Aristotle (who asserted in his *Poetics* that when it comes to plotting a plausible impossibility is preferable to an unconvincing possibility) to back his hand Chandler makes a double-bluff virtue of necessity by having Marlowe explicitly comment on this far-fetchedness coming to pass. The fetch is not sourced from so far away as that of the *The High Window* and simply because we want there to be a story anyway I believe Chandler is home and free on this one.

Where he has nothing but the quickness and terseness of his action to help him – Aristotle is certainly no use here – is during the plotting hodge-podge he bodges together so as to orchestrate Marlowe's having to enter into that one-on-one jeopardy with Degarmo.

It happens thus. The narrative three parts done, Marlowe's client receives a phone call from his wife – the wife who absconded over a month before and whom Marlowe was engaged to trace. Allegedly off to secure a quickie divorce and a new husband she says that she is back in Los Angeles and urgently in need of $500 in notes. She designates a rendezvous. The client asks Marlowe to courier the money to her. After demurring at first Marlowe eventually agrees.

Now. One: it was early established that the bolting wife had more than ample funds of her own. Two: there is no earthly reason why Marlowe should be the one conveying the money. Three:

there is no earthly reason why the woman who has actually met Marlowe before in somewhat bizarre circumstances should know that he will be the courier. The two meet in a hotel room. A conversation ensues which contains a great deal of plot explanation and makes clear beyond any doubt that the woman is not the wife of Marlowe's client. But the exchange is abruptly broken off. Marlowe has walked into Four: a (presumably hastily improvised) trap. He is knocked unconscious by a third party hidden in the room. In comparatively short order Marlowe comes round. He is still in the room – as is the woman. She has been murdered, however, and to a degree has been sexually molested. Marlowe has been left alive presumably to become prime suspect for the crime although, Five: this begs the question as to how he received a semi-serious injury on the back of his head. It also, Six: leaves us to wonder in due course why he was not simply eliminated along with the woman. Somebody tries the door to the room. Seven: the police have neglected to obtain a key before ascending to the room. Now, Eight: Chandler is obliged to inflict upon Marlowe an escapade unique in the canon. He has him break out of a bathroom window and work his way along Spiderman fashion to the corresponding window in the adjacent room (conveniently vacant) and break back inside. All this six floors above ground. In short, Chandler has reduced Marlowe down to the puerile status of Bruce Willis in one of those ineffably boring 'action movies' in which John McClain meets another gang who can't shoot straight. Only the fact that Marlowe fails to make good his escape from the police when he tries exiting the second room offers any sliver of redemption for this descent into comic book expediency.

Well. We have been here before. Once again it is a reader being wise after the event: a considerably while after the event. Scrutinising the episode in the literary morgue as it hangs suspended in the formaldehyde like an example of Damien Hirst's lab assistant technology, we can shake our heads. But, not so incredibly when given our past experiences, the entire sequence 'plays'. As we read, we suspend disbelief.

The truth is that within minutes of finishing a Marlowe story we are beginning to forget the 'who did what to whom' mechanics. What remains is the remembered sense of pleasure we have derived from the smooth deployment of apt words and structured paragraphs, vivid description, telling images, incisive characterisations, gnomic commentary that have graced the pages. And, beyond, as we lay aside a Chandler book we are left for a while, at least, with the warm sense that in a wicked, wicked world it is still possible to navigate and contend without surrendering all sense of personal honour and even to survive a touch enhanced by the struggle. The streamlined morality of Chandler's thriller melodrama gives us a fast-track stimulus to revive and revisit our own better instincts.

How many revitalised anythings Chandler himself had by the time he completed *The Lady in the Lake* is less than crystal clear. Very few, if any, probably. He had been on the treadmill for four novels straight now and almost certainly off the wagon for at least half that grinding time. Where to now, though? What next? The same difference all over again? Not so easy when the backlog of short stories recycling for the use of was looking so depleted. God, he could do with a break. But needs must when the rent book, yet again, and Cissy's increasingly bad health were calling the treadmill tune. Then, in the spring of 1943, from out of the blue, like a stretched stroke of fortune in a Marlowe plot, a phone call came. A Mr Sistrom, a film producer.

Whatever Chandler's needs for income, a change of work pattern, an increase in alcohol consumption, help was at hand. Hollywood help. Paramount was coming down the pike prepared to simplify his problems by intensifying them.

Chandler in Hollywood

THE DAY AFTER THE PUBLICATION OF *Childe Harold* Byron awoke to find himself famous. In 1943 with *The Big Sleep*, *Farewell, My Lovely* and *The High Window* out upon the world Chandler discerned himself still largely obscure. It was true that he had sold the screen rights of the latter two to the studios, but it had been for the token amounts B pictures dispensed. More seriously, now in his mid-fifties, he was feeling jaded, written out.

A contemporary author who had awoken to fame was James Cain. He had been high in the bestseller lists for much of the thirties and otherwise regardless the major studios had snapped up his titles – to buy themselves immediate problems. The Hays Office still held iron sway over Hollywood's subject matter. Today we tend to think of its Production Code as callowly prudish: films should be made for the Hardy families who took their apple pie with ice cream and whose homes were never darkened by a double bed crossing the threshold. But there was another side to the

Code. As far as the Hays Office was concerned America was a country without a Klan, a Mafia, corrupt politicians, industrial strife, inadequate health care, bad John Does. The vein of melodramatic, going on 'sordid', sexually-explicit realism that Cain worked meant that throughout the latter 1930s the Hollywood 'properties' *The Postman Always Rings Twice* and *Mildred Pierce* remained unmade.

This did not entirely deter one producer at Paramount, Joe Sistrom. Already a fan, he had come upon a 1936 Cain magazine serial, *Double Indemnity*. The story of an adulterous wife who induces her lover to murder her husband for the insurance money, it was dark, certainly, it would need a lot of finessing to get past the Code, but, hell, life wasn't all Betty Grable and Dick Haymes. Cynical Billy Wilder would consider it right down his *strasse*. He would see it as a *Thérèse Raquin* story of just plain folks. The hell of it was, though, that Cain was tied up at Warner's. And Charlie Brackett, Wilder's sparring partner (sic!) on recent screenplays was refusing outright to become involved this time on a project whose subject matter was so 'disgusting'. Hmmn ... Who could they bring in to help sanitize the screenplay?

Unknown to many though he still might be, Chandler did have an admirer in Sistrom. The producer arranged a meeting. As a result one of the classic, black, 'Odd Couple' marriages that were to characterize Wilder's entire Hollywood career became arranged.

The initial meeting set the farcical tone. Chandler needing a change of pace and glad as a Los Angeleno to stumble upon a local employer was basically positive in outlook. But Wilder and Sistrom were taken right aback by his age – twenty years, at least, more than they had expected. Wilder cruelly, but no doubt

Wilder-Chandler partnership may have been end-to-end purgatory but there had, eventually, been a marriage of two talents.

And then some more. Barbara Stanwyck may have had a few equals but America has never produced a more versatilely superior screen actress. Forty-six years later Billy Wilder publicly pronounced her to be 'the best I ever worked with.' When, reading the screenplay she realized that Phyllis Dietrichson would allow her to translate her erstwhile Lady Eve into a bourgeois Lady Macbeth, her heart must have leapt with joy.

Fred MacMurray, however, came by the role of Walter Neff by default. He was not at the time one of Paramount's leading men. But none of Hollywood's eye-and-teeth, alleged top-drawer male stars had any desire to sully their box office ratings by playing an ordinary Joe, who having turned into an adulterer killer, pays for it with his own life. George Raft, praises be, rejected the part. (He didn't want middle America to think him a bad guy!)

MacMurray had the same reservations. He had built a comfortable career playing the easy-going guy next door who might come on a little fresh occasionally but was basically as pleasant a straight-shooter as the home town day was long. But, as we now can appreciate, MacMurray was never better on film – *The Caine Mutiny, The Apartment* – than when playing a heel. And Wilder, knowing the typical MacMurray performances, sensing the potential, knew he would make a perfect Neff. So he does. For the first ten minutes or so he allows us to see the nice, even charming, guy waiting to get out from behind the sales-talk patter. But, alas, the charm, the fast-talking wit, are on a street-wise level. Deep down, once Phyllis Dietrichson has thrown his switch, he's dumb. It is only when the scales fall from his eyes that his better, more intelligent self can assert itself. And by then, he knows, it is too late. MacMurray's perfectly-weighted performance – smart-mouthed modulating to smart-aleck to contritely wised-up is masterly. He makes of Walter Neff an *American Tragedy* writ smaller but far more persuasive.

This prompts a detouring thought. None of the major screen Marlowes – Bogart, Powell, Montgomery, Gould, Garner, Mitchum – have quite caught Chandler's original. I am inclined to suggest that MacMurray, glammed up a touch in a downbeat way by makeup and wardrobe, could have parlayed his charm and way with a one-liner into giving us the portrayal most satisfyingly close to Chandler's own conception. William Holden fans are at liberty to disagree.

The top brass at Paramount viewed the answer print of the final version of *Double Indemnity* and knowingly prepared to face the derision this turkey would generate. Instead, when premiered the film won virtually unanimous critical acclaim and was an overnight box-office success. It garnered five nominations for Academy Awards and has commanded the same respect and admiration unbrokenly for close to seventy years. One of its greatest admirers was James Cain. In due course he came to say:

> It's the only picture I ever saw made from my books that had things in it I wish I had thought of.

Though it was only the second of many still to come, I am inclined to believe that *Double Indemnity* endures as the best film Wilder made. I think this is so because he concentrated his talent and vision on making them serve the immediate needs within the tight parameters of the narrative. The later films tend towards the ostentatiously significant (*Sunset Boulevard*), the coarsely complacent (*A Foreign Affair*), the knowingly slick, 'Look at me, Ma!' indulgent (*Some Like it Hot*). At times, for all their many virtues, these films cause us to think that Wilder's eye is not on the material but the gallery who are just going to eat up their next little directorial master-stroke. Some critics simply reject Wilder's mordantly cynical interpretation of life. I rather think he got this right. What I consider his Achilles' heel is his propensity towards the short-term glib. Since he is such a good director technically in terms of knowing where to put the camera looking at what through which lens, I find him extraordinarily difficult to place in terms of the great Pantheon in the sky. But when, staying within the boundaries of the United States, I call to mind Keaton, Hawks, Welles, Sturges, I find myself of the opinion that glibness is insufficiently close to genius.

Double Indemnity proved to be much more than just a very good and successful film. It became a highly influential one. It had forced open a side door in the Production Code's censorious, sanitizing ring-fence. And Hollywood had seen that there were big bucks in these 'bad taste' properties. Now *Mildred Pierce* and *The Postman Always Rings Twice* went into production and on to profitable release. And the brew was thickening. Films such as *Cornered* and *Dead Reckoning* were beginning to percolate into the melodramatic thriller genre an awareness that there was something distinctly 'black' about contemporary life. It didn't make headlines but everyone knew that America was full of men returned from the war to a land palpably fit neither for heroes nor for plain GI Joes with their nerves shot to pieces. Films that were more than just crime capers began to appear – the splendid *Crossfire, Body and Soul*, the peerlessly elegiac *Out of the Past, Force of Evil*, incredibly, and in due course, *The Sound of Fury* (so shamefully neglected) and *In a Lonely Place*. It is not a great exaggeration to suggest that Chandler's dialogue put into the hands of Wilder permitted *Double Indemnity* to blaze a dark trail for such fine and lastingly valuable movies as these.

Sadly, even though one of the five Academy Award nominations *Double Indemnity* had received was for its screenplay, the two co-writers never worked together again. Sad but inevitable. Neither of the two would have repined. Most likely, after all the hurtling insults and put-downs, the volleys of jabs and counter-jabs, they never spoke again. But Time cauterizes the wounds. Chandler could claim that it was pretty good for a rookie on his first entry to find himself up for an Oscar. But he would have had no doubt as to whom the greater credit must go. Five years later in a letter to Hamish Hamilton he could cast a cold eye and apportion the credit along with the blame.

> Working with Billy Wilder on *Double Indemnity* was an agonizing experience and has probably shortened my life, but I learned from it about as much about screenwriting as I am capable of learning, which is not very much …

Enough maybe. The Paramount execs now realized that in their far-seeing wisdom they had managed to hire in under their roof a (currently) sought-after talent. They proceeded to make him an offer he couldn't refuse. Money tends to dissipate agony. Chandler decided he could handle being wealthy. He decided to go on drinking his lunch in this town. Wilder, meanwhile, was busy on the preparation for his next project, *The Lost Weekend*. It is, let us not forget, an in-depth study of a chronic alcoholic.

After the penny-pinching semi-reclusive years in the outer circles of Los Angeles, Chandler initially enjoyed the congeniality of the Paramount commissariat. (In particular, according to some accounts, he enjoyed the extra-curricular congeniality of a certain Paramount secretary.) His first two routine staff assignments were to administer screenplay doctoring resuscitation to scripts already terminally doomed. Speedily, though, he was presented with a one-off challenge worthy of his potential.

The war in the Pacific was dragging on. In some three months Paramount's blue-chip star Alan Ladd was scheduled to be re-drafted. The studio chiefs wanted a picture to be rushed through that could milk them profit from his high-riding box-office popularity. At this very juncture Chandler, his first contract completed, was in the early stages of an agent-negotiated original screenplay that allowed him a personal office at Paramount. He offered to convert this work in early progress into an Alan Ladd vehicle.

The producer saddled with the express delivery was the erudite and cultured and also English-educated John Housman. He jumped at Chandler's offer. But then things stalled. Chandler, locked in that office alone, the clock ticking, developed writer's block. He decided, at whatever personal cost, to quit. But school-tie *noblesse oblige* played up and played the game. Public school chaps don't let each other down. Reversing his first U-turn Chandler said that there might be a desperate way forward.

If he could work from home the script might yet get done. Housman, as Orson Welles' Mercury Theatre *fidus Achates* was well used to crises and expedients. Agreeing, he laid on round the clock hot and cold running relays of typists and limos. Both men knew that Chandler's going back on the sauce in earnest would probably doom any last chance he had of boxing a draw with his drinking problem. But the devil was driving … Chandler was found at all hours slumped blind drunk over his own typewriter but with more pages scattered around. The script was finished. It emerged being just about worth the sacrifice.

The Blue Dahlia was made a viable project by *Double Indemnity*'s ice-breaking attenuation of the Production Code. Perfect for Alan Ladd's slender talent, it is not a Betty Grable vehicle. It is a precursor of *Crossfire*.

The setting is LA (easy for Chandler, easy for Ladd). Three soldiers are back from overseas on the point of discharge. Home free, then. Not exactly. One of them, Buzz, has come close to dying. He now has a steel plate in his skull replacing the bone removed by the shrapnel. What he has inside his skull is more problematic. Buzz is given to drinking heavily. He suffers blind drunk blackouts and memory loss. He panics into huge and instant fits of rage. In the finished film Buzz is played by William Bendix, as prodigiously talented and technically assured an actor as ever graced Hollywood. He delivers an amazingly rounded and sympathetic performance that embodies the (then unspoken) fate of countless returning GIs. It scorches away the bad syrupy taste left in the mouth by Goldwyn's *Best Years of Our Lives*. This is evident in the film's opening, arguably best, scene.

The three returnees are in a bar. The juke box is playing big band jazz – loudly. Buzz flares up at this 'monkey music' beating up on him inside his head. He pulls the plug on the box. A fourth veteran is as instantly incensed at having his nickel's worth cut short. A fight is one more insult away. Only Ladd's diplomatic intervention prevents it starting – that and the fourth veteran's realizing that the big loudmouth asking for trouble is more than that. Touchingly he realizes that this is a brother-in-arms who has sustained on-going damage. Violence is averted.

Not for long. That night Ladd's tramp of a wife is found murdered. Buzz had gone off on a sustained drinking bout, had been seen at the scene of the crime, now has no memory of what happened. He is the obvious and prime suspect.

The story-line now settles down along conventional lines. The Ladd character becomes the *de facto* Private Eye, sifting the evidence to discover who really did commit the murder. We have moved into whodunnit territory. In due course we find out whether or not it was the butler.

In Chandler's original draft it was not the butler. The killer proves to be Buzz. He was not, of course, responsible for this terrible action which he genuinely cannot remember. The war was. Chandler was using the conventional format as a Trojan horse in which to pack a most disquieting suggestion.

The first version never happened. The Hollywood, and still more the Military, establishment were never going to go public at Alan Ladd-level on the truth that when Johnny came marching home he might well need to be treated as other than a conquering hero. This was a time when John Huston's harrowing documentary recording of a traumatized soldier breaking down on camera, *Let There Be Light,* was officially consigned to deepest outer darkness.

George Marshall – the filmmaker, not the general – was a

competent director. He even got a passable performance out of the actress whom Chandler took to referring to as Moronica Lake. The film still passes entertaining muster. But what a missed opportunity. Given Bendix's massive talent, a faithful realization of Chandler's first conception might have given us a major film of genuinely tragic dimension.

Post-traumatic Stress Disorder was not a term in 1940s usage. It was scarcely a condition that was recognized. Now we know better. Some people knew better then. It is there in Remarque's 1929 novel. I would wager, if not my house, a frightening amount on it being there in Chandler.

He was in the same First World War trenches as Remarque, and all but blown to kingdom come there. It was during convalescence and his subsequent period as a trainee pilot – an almost certain death sentence at the time – that he discovered his propensity for, his short-term tolerance of, alcohol on a binge drinking scale. Black outs, memory loss – I believe Buzz and Chandler are also brothers-in-arms and that there is something grimly ironic, heroic even, about the vision of Chandler tackling his demons head on over his typewriter and another near-emptied fifth of bourbon. With cynical hindsight we might say that the best long-term outcome of *The Blue Dahlia* booze-fuelled blitzkrieg is that it served in morning-after time permanently to sour Chandler's illusions (if any) about Hollywood and the alleged craft of screenwriting. By now he had spent some of his hard-earned Paramount money on buying that mint-new house on that part of the Southern California coast which he and Cissy had long coveted as a place to settle in. Possibly the unprecedented sense of owning his own home and thus, though not in

Bloomsbury, possessing a room of his own influenced him. It may have been an allied sense that if he made his home his castle it could be one with a figurative ivory tower. But, his thoughts were now turned back to joined up writing: to prose. To the novel and to Marlowe.

It was not an instant return to yesterday. He still had commitments to Paramount. He had proved a money maker for them and they were prepared to cut him a lot of slack if it would get the best from him. He made token efforts to respond. Projects were begun, scripts started. But enervated, jaded, disillusioned, inebriated, the spirit and flesh alike were weak. All dribbled away into the sand and recrimination. Paramount suspended him. Fences were mended. In vain. In due course he went out of the iconic gate for the last time.

Subsequently he had just two formal involvements with the film industry. In 1950 Hitchcock was interested in inveigling Chandler to adapt a property he was intending to bring to the screen. It was history revisited. The book was *Strangers on a Train* and, as with *Double Indemnity* (though for different reasons) there was no way the original author would be doing the adaptation. Further, Hitchcock uncomfortably represented a return to Wilder. He too, though a lesser (in my opinion) talent was a confrontational, egocentric bully, and no less suspect on the screen of going for the short-term, glib, self-congratulatory 'cinematic' effect. Still, Hitchcock ...

Playing hard to get Chandler agreed to the proposal on the basis, again, that he could work from home. Hitchcock would have to motor down Routes One and Five for all working sessions. The great man did. But not for long. Chandler began work but speedily found that Hitchcock's emphasis from the word go on 'business' and mood jarred with his own concern to evolve an organically plausible and consistent narrative. He voiced his irritation at the time in a letter to Hamish Hamilton again:

> The thing that amuses me [sic] about Hitchcock is the way he directs a film in his head before he knows what the story is. You find yourself trying to rationalize the shots he wants to make rather than the story. Every time you get set he jabs you off balance by wanting to do a love scene on top of the Jefferson Memorial.

Hitchcock, for his part, may have become increasingly uncomfortably aware of the gulf between Dulwich and the East End, for Chandler, whether amused or not, was taking a leaf out of Wilder's book and was becoming openly rude. Ultimately, his heart and brain not in it any more, he chose the morning of yet another Hitchcock arrival audibly to refer to him as a 'fat bastard' as the director got out of his car. That was pretty much that.

Chandler asked not to receive any credit when *Strangers on a Train* was eventually released and his verdict on the film was stark and simple: 'no guts, no characters, no dialogue.' It would seem that his system was not entirely free of 'fat bastard' poisoning.

Earlier, however, in 1947-8, left to his own creative devices Chandler had delivered himself of a complete and original script. His agent had negotiated a deal with Universal, a studio on the edge of Poverty Row. Chandler responded with a screenplay loosely in the key of *The Blue Dahlia*. Its point of departure was an actual quirk in American jurisprudence – a one-off State law upheld in North Carolina. Chandler called his handiwork *Playback*.

Universal's top brass liked the screenplay but never went ahead with its production. They were staring down the barrel of bankruptcy right then. *Playback,* for necessary plot purposes, had to be shot on location in Seattle close to the Washington State/British Columbia border: that would make the production costs prohibitively expensive. The project was shelved. Handsomely paid himself, Chandler no doubt chalked the exercise up to experience and set about forgetting it. He had already indicated to Alfred Knopf that he was bent on another Marlowe story.

Chandler's time in Tinseltown may have severely sabotaged his career as a novelist and robbed us of several fine books. Equally, it may just as well have given him a change of pace which, however hectic and lurid, did eventually renew his appetite for the study and the long-haul, page-by-page writing of fiction. Who can presume to judge? Hollywood certainly did give him raw material for use in his work downstream. It is likely, I personally feel, that his work as a fully committed screenplay author would have shown a decline. I suspect that his own final judgment on his Hollywood experience (in a 1951 letter) represents a canny and accurate summing up:

> A preoccupation with words for their own sake is fatal to good film making. It's not what films are for. It's not my cup of tea, but it could have been if I'd started it twenty years earlier. But twenty years earlier of course I could never have got there, and that is true of a great many people. They don't want you until you have made a name and by the time you have made a name you have developed some kind of talent they can't use. All they will do is spoil it, if you let them.

In vino, perhaps, *veritas.*

The Long Goodbye

WHICHEVER OF THE FIVE NOVELS CHANDLER published between 1939 and 1949 deserves to be any given individual's favourite is likely to be disputed with amiable ferocity by literally millions of the others who have read these books over the past half century. But all readers to the last man and woman will be united in one fundamental opinion. All five differ only in degree. The one or the other may seem to possess a hint of superior pace or plausibility, sharper wit, more engrossing characters, more casually seductive prose. But however much such qualities may vary, if at all, page to page, chapter to chapter, all of the first five Marlowe books are not only of the same genre, they are all, give or take some occasional transpositions, in the same key. I think, however, that in the case of the sixth book, *The Long Goodbye*, published in 1954, such an assertion can no longer be confidently maintained.

This may appear at first glance a thoroughly contentious remark. After all, the building blocks of *The Long Goodbye* would seem to be identical to those of the earlier thrillers. Once again we have the spectrum of indifferent and cynically honourable cops. Two Mr Big-style gangster bosses feature in the plot line, both, to varying degrees, possessed of a certain class and style and underworld honour. Various alluring, seductive and enigmatic women are dressed into the action. We meet another multi-millionaire with more money and influence than sense or personal fulfilment. And, in a work written during the twilight last years of Cissy Chandler's own sadly long goodbye, we are presented perhaps not entirely by chance with a veritable rogue's gallery of Southern California's snake-oil medicos – one of whom is the unctuously profiteering proprietor of a hospice for geriatrics.

Absolutely the usual suspects then, we might reasonably think: *plus ça change*. And, indeed, reviving his interim habit again, Chandler went all the way back to one of his earlier pulp stories to kick-start this new work and, we might suspect, himself. The opening of *The Long Goodbye* is that of 'The Curtain' writ longer and the first major event in the novel's narrative is an aborted intention in the short story now played out in full.

Given this slew of identical constituents it shares with its five novel-length predecessors it would be reasonable to assume that *The Long Goodbye* must be a direct continuation in kind of the thriller genre. Yet this has never seemed to me to be quite the case. With stealthily growing force my first reading of what was in any case clearly Chandler's longest work to date increased an impression in me of a change in tone of voice significantly modifying the, shall we say, routine formula. Years later I discovered this impression to be largely justified. In 1952 when

Chandler sent his New York agency a first draft of *The Long Goodbye* it was accompanied by an explanatory letter.

> It has been clear to me for some time that what is largely boring about mystery stories, at least on a literate plain, is that the characters get lost about a third of the way through. Often the opening, the *mise en scène*, the establishment of the background is very good. Then the plot thickens and the people become mere names. Well what can you do to avoid this? You can write constant action and that is fine if you really enjoy it. But alas one grows up, one becomes complicated and unsure, one becomes interested in moral dilemmas, rather than in who cracked who on the head ... Anyhow I wrote this as I wanted because I can do that now. I didn't care *whether the mystery was fairly obvious*, but I cared about the people, about this strange corrupt world we live in, and how any man who tried to be honest, looks in the end either sentimental or plain foolish.

Nineteen fifty-two was also the year that Chandler took the dying Cissy to England on a slow boat eastbound through the Panama Canal. (Rather than recruit her strength, alas, the voyage exacerbated her condition: she returned home the weaker.) But in the course of that first draft Marlowe, by Chandler's explicit design, had already experienced his own sea change.

It is, in part, a question of wavelength. *The Long Goodbye* is deployed by means of an ampler, more generous frequency that comes to us more steadily. There is no staccato. The criss-crossing, double-crossing, cat's-cradling flurry of incidents that mark the earlier books is almost entirely absent. It is not until late in the narrative that anything resembling guys coming through the door with guns in their hands occurs – and even then the menace is conflated into something lengthier and more subtle than a quick scare-the-pants-off-you diversion from a plotting weakness. *The Long Goodbye* is played out courtesy of a simple linear construction that is not afraid to take its paratactic time. It travels past us like a steadily moving train made up of a few but lengthy carriages. These sections couple together thus.

The narrative begins with Marlowe, quite by chance, coming across a totally incapable drunk in that most universal of limbos, a parking lot. He rescues the drunk, a Terry Lennox, from major embarrassment and, soon after, a second predicament and, Lennox proving to be a flawlessly well-mannered Scott Fitzgerald of an alcoholic, the two form an incipient friendship. Then things take a darker turn. Lennox, whose face bears the distinct scars of extensive plastic surgery, seems for all his charm, a fecklessly hollow man. Quite possibly he suffers from mental scarring too. He turns up on Marlowe's doorstep one pre-dawn morning and, plainly in desperate straits, asks Marlowe to drive him south to Tijuana across the Mexican border. Marlowe obliges.

This third favour initiates the second phase of the novel. Immediately on his return to Los Angeles Marlowe is picked up by the police. Lennox's wife has been found brutally beaten to death. Who else could have done it other than the husband who has fled? They know Marlowe helped him run. They want to know the chapter and verse details.

The Long Goodbye is the first Marlowe novel that does not begin with the detective formally accepting a commission. Thus, under police interrogation, he cannot now refuse to answer on the grounds of protecting his client's confidentiality. Nevertheless, pushing the law to its limits he refuses to divulge the details the police are after. This results in his undergoing the severest grilling and man-handling Chandler ever exposes him to but, toughing it out, Marlowe stays tight-lipped. Eventually the law (and perhaps somebody's influence) somehow operating in his favour, the police have no recourse but to release him from custody. This would seem only to be a temporary respite; but then matters are simplified by the news of Lennox having committed suicide in Mexico. *Finita la commedia.* Marlowe is back on the streets again, his reputation somewhat begrudgedly enhanced in the eyes of a handful of hard men on either side of the law. There are a few instances of curious fallout. One of the said hard men, an LA mobster, braces Marlowe in his office, warning him – quite unnecessarily – not to try to make any capital out of his knowledge of Lennox's last days. A letter, a pre-suicide note from Lennox, arrives from Mexico. It contains a huge 'token of esteem', retroactive payment-cum-gratuity.

The narrative's third block is largely concerned with exposition and would seem at first to mark a new beginning. It finds Marlowe back accepting (or rejecting) penny-ante assignments on the level of tracing runaway husbands. Then comes an off-beat request from a New York publisher who has flown across the country to make it in person. His firm publishes the works of a bestselling, but nevertheless possibly talented, Los Angeles-based writer who has ground to a halt with his next blockbuster unfinished. The immediate impediment to any continuation is the writer Roger Wade's utter dedication to drinking himself into alcoholic oblivion. Marlowe turns down the request on the grounds that he isn't in business as a male nurse. The publisher replies that

Marlowe's task will be to try to uncover the reason *behind* Wade's compulsive drinking. Marlowe still demurs but when, in artfully oblique fashion, Wade's wife Eileen, a woman more glowingly described than any other in the Chandler canon, joins the conversation, he provisionally agrees to meet with Wade. When, later, he learns from Eileen Wade that her husband has been missing on a bender for three days, he senses that this is something more tangible for him to get to grips with.

Pragmatically putting to use his workaday skills Marlowe is able to track down the missing author and rescue him from virtual imprisonment in – naturally! – a dubiously less than legal 'sanatorium'. The incident serves to conjure up much the same relationship between Marlowe and Roger Wade that Marlowe previously shared with Terry Lennox – a guarded mutual respect and another incipient friendship. Certainly, albeit socially rather than professionally, Marlowe now has the *entrée* to the Wade's luxurious Idle Valley home.

It is only now when Marlowe has leisure to interact with the Wades that the narrative of *The Long Goodbye* ceases to advance on a 'one thing after another' basis. Marlowe begins to discern that the edgy, unstable, potentially violent marriage of his new acquaintances may have acquired its fault lines in the past. Roger Wade may have drunk himself into a deliberate oblivion less to escape his sense of inadequacy as a writer than to achieve a memory black-out of incidents he cannot bear to remember and live with. Eileen Wade, for all her ethereal beauty, also seems at times not to be living in the here and now. As a young woman she was trapped in London during the blitz. She there had some involvement with a young soldier killed in action. His memory still haunts her. One evening, in a trance-like zombie state she attempts to seduce Marlowe offering herself with a literally naked directness. It is as much the diversion caused by the Wade's threateningly touchy house-boy as his own sense of honour that avoids her offer being accepted up to the hilt.

It is now, as the narrative begins to loop back to the past, that another woman enters Marlowe's life. For old times' sake he has gone to a bar – their joint favourite joint – to drink a farewell toast to the dead Lennox. The drink of choice will be a gimlet – Lennox's favourite tipple. An elegant woman is already ensconced at the bar with this same off-beat choice of drink. She is there and drinking it because she too knew Lennox. It is a small world.

It is indeed. This woman, a Linda Loring, is the sister of the woman whose brutal beating to a pulp caused her husband, Terry Lennox, to flee the country and then kill himself. And Linda Loring's own husband is Eileen Wade's personal physician. Before long such of these people who are still alive find themselves together at a cocktail party (improbably) thrown by the Wades. A new element which Chandler now factors in to the narrative is that Dr Loring is a self-regarding chateau-bottled shit.

At last then, *The Long Goodbye* arrives at a cat's-cradling. But only of sorts. It is not driven by, as it were, tangible devices – planted evidence, substituted fingerprints, phony shake-downs – as by the psychological ricocheting to and fro between the major protagonists. Marlowe is both participant and observer in this process which encompasses two significant events. The one is spending the night thoroughly satisfactorily with Dr Loring's wife before declining to join her either in Paris or marriage. The second is the violent death of Roger Wade.

ego he might have become if he had not buckled down to forging a new career for himself as a writer and enduring the years of desk-bound grind that necessarily followed. This was an act of dogged willpower that the fictional Terry Lennox is not capable of emulating. This is why, when, disguised, he returns to LA to thank Marlowe and, as he hopes, renew their fledgling, thoroughly amiable friendship, Marlowe rejects him. However charming, Lennox is indeed too lightweight. Like Blanche Dubois before him he has taken to going through life depending too much upon the kindness of strangers. But if he is never going to help himself then Marlowe is not prepared to indulge him permanently. He gives it to Lennox straight.

> 'Don't worry about it, Terry. There's always somebody around to do it for you.'
> 'I was in the Commandos, bud. They don't take you if you're just a piece of fluff. I got badly hurt and it wasn't any fun with those Nazi doctors. It did something to me.'
> 'I know all that, Terry. You're a very sweet guy in a lot of ways. I'm not judging you. I never did. It's just that you're not here any more. You're long gone. You've got nice clothes and perfume and you're as elegant as a fifty-dollar whore.'
> 'That's just an act,' he said almost desperately.
> 'You get a kick out of it, don't you?'

Marlowe *is* judging him. As is Chandler. I would hazard that in 1953, Cissy still alive, this long novel just sentences away from completion, Chandler felt capable of saying 'Get thee behind me' to the hollow *alter ego* he had managed to avoid becoming in the past and would hope not to inhabit in the future.

Chandler's putative relationship with the other spectacular drunkard in *The Long Goodbye* is even more marked because Roger Wade is an author. He is, indeed, a hugely bestselling author and, as such, a valuable commercial asset to his publishers. Immediately he is no worth at all to them because he is suffering from that writer's block. Marlowe's initial encounter with Wade arises out of the publishing house's wish to 'unblock' this golden goose – either by having him weaned away from his alcohol intake or, the profounder thought, by tracing and eliminating whatever underlying anxiety is lodged in Wade's mind, and driving him to drink. 'Lodged in his subconscious' would be the better way to express this aim. A key foreground element of the plotting in *The Long Goodbye* is that, a central figure in the social set that also included the openly promiscuous adultress who has now been brutally beaten to death, Wade has so blacked out that, like *The Blue Dahlia*'s Buzz, he is not able to remember how he relates to her murder. We surmise that either he cannot remember whether he was responsible and, alcohol assisted, is suppressing all memory of his crime, or that he is innocent but, knowing the identity of the true killer, is trying to expunge his accessory's knowledge instead. He might, of course, be faking his lack of recall.

Wade has a second reason for his inclination to go on benders. His books sell like hot cakes, yes, and the royalties roll in, but a discerning voice inside tells him they are worthless. Since we have been told his genre is the swordplay-packed bodice ripper we cannot but think that the interior voice is most probably correct. Nor has it gone entirely unheeded. Alerted by Wade's intelligent and observant wife, Marlowe has come upon a page or two fresh from Wade's typewriter where, it would seem, somewhere between drunken stupor and bestseller hackdom he has made a conscious effort to change his literary DNA.

Marlowe finds himself reading something a long way from gadzookery and pistols at dawn. Trying to get in touch with his genuinely creative inner man Wade has spewed forth two or three pages that could only have been written in the late 1950s – a sub-Joycean, Kerouacesque stream of self-conscious consciousness such as a mildly talented sophomore in a Creative Writing class might have pastiched. In terms of the foreground narrative again, these pages – they break off abruptly, incomplete – are possibly significant. Read between the lines they could be taken as an oblique confession by Wade that he did indeed murder Lennox's wife. Then again, given the deluge of self-loathing they display and the note of deep despair they abruptly break off on, they might be taken as the prelude to a suicide note. But accessed for their own inherent worth these pages, I think, make it plain enough that as a practising writer, Roger Wade would have been far better off confining himself to the 1750s.

I think we have to award Chandler very high marks here. If we consider that in trying on the character of Wade for size by means of this fictional template Chandler was seeking directly to express himself and get in touch with his own literary inner man, then this 'contemporary' passage would be nothing but an embarrassment. But Chandler was subtler and more intelligent than that. He gives us from Wade's typewriter exactly the derivative pinchbeck that a hack writer with ideas above his talent might have produced out of a sudden hung-over fit of energy in that Southern Californian place at that time. Not that the 'placing' of Wade's talent ever becomes a key issue in *The Long Goodbye*.

The relevance of this passage lies in the fact that in due course Marlowe finds Wade shot dead with a gun at his side, indeed an apparent suicide.

I am sometimes tempted to wonder whether Chandler missed a cute trick in attributing to Wade his particular literary niche. What if instead of making him a purveyor of historical romances he had made him a writer of hard-boiled thrillers? Might this not have opened the door on to some very piquant exchanges between Wade and Marlowe?

Very dangerous territory, indeed. To begin with and on the surface level it would demand of Marlowe (sardonically pointing up Wade's procedural errors), a greater level of truly authentic expertise than Chandler – though perhaps not Hammett – could probably have given him. At a deeper level such a 'conceit' would have risked appearing thoroughly pretentious. The thought that Chandler was toying with translating himself into Pirandello would have fleered up between reader and text puncturing the integrity of the novel's world and grinding the narrative's momentum to a halt. Most deeply of all the 'conceit' of Wade being a thriller writer would have come across as exactly that in our modern use of the word. It would have seemed self-referential to the point of being incestuous – far too cloyingly close to La Jolla home. Wade as an unambiguous surrogate for Chandler would have made of *The Long Goodbye* an insufferable wallow. Chandler possessed far too much literary tact as to wear his ego on his sleeve so indulgently.

In this regard I need to insert a cautionary note at this point – even a self-admonition. None of this grade-school 'analysis' (aka juvenile psycho-babble) on the subject of Chandler conveying himself into the body of *The Long Goodbye* on the back of its three principal male characters has any direct bearing on the operation of the book *qua* book. Within the confine of the text those three characters execute their function with a completely self-engendered fulfilment that has no need of secondary information imported from outside. An English-speaking Vulcan, finding a copy of *The Long Goodbye* among the rubble three centuries hence, will be able to read it and enjoy it exactly as we now read *The Odyssey*. My speculations as to how the characters of Philip Marlowe, Terry Lennox and Roger Wade may have evolved out of Chandler's own psyche are not concerned with the performance or quality of the end product but with the springs of its creation.

If it is true that *The Long Goodbye* 'plays', that it stands self-sufficiently on its own two feet, because of Chandler's literary discretion, then I believe that we are contemplating a very important consideration as regards that artefact known as the novel.

A huge proportion of fiction – perhaps the preponderance – has its source in, and is fuelled by, autobiography. Authors believe a theme or situation provides abiding interest because it is significant to themselves in their flesh-and-blood lives. It is not necessarily so. Without the thousand and one processes that go into transmuting raw experience and observation into a shaped, *self-sufficient* work of art in which all gels to achieve an outward-looking universality, the attitude 'this really happened to me so it has to be a matter of interest to everyone else' is wishful thinking. Such universality is only arrived at when, ceasing to be an oblique journal, the novel becomes free-standing through an interior logic deriving from fully-realised, thought-through characters inhabiting the freshly-minted, achieved landscape of this new attempt to distil art from everyday existence.

This is hard work. So many writers redeploying personal experience on the page fail to bear down enough. Their recollections may indeed be freighted with huge import for themselves but if they fail in the design of their novel and the immediate precision of their words to plant characters and situations in contexts that are vividly concrete enough to convey their *raison d'être* in the narrative, we will not share the given author's original sensations but only be given a bulletin that lists them. The narrative will not be of universal significance. If the author's sense of self is so overwhelming as to make him or her attach vast importance to what is in any case essentially commonplace we may find ourselves reading a very bad book indeed as the lists proliferate toward the crack of doom.

On which subject a primary pitfall lying in wait for the progress of any author-centric novel is the phenomenon that because each setting, each character, each new reach of the narrative is rich in significance for the writer, he or she assumes this significance is blindingly obvious to the reader. Simply to mention the new issue is to convey its import. Bad autobiographical novels thus so often settle down to offering the reader a monotonously regular drip-feed of exposition and explanation as their writers flatly report all that they wish to convey in a tone of voice and from a point of view that lack all variation. Told this, that and the other for a fact, the reader is not asked to deduce or anticipate. The reader is seldom presented with the inscrutable or the ambiguous as the omniscient author tells all once and for all.

Chandler, be it noted, never does this. Although the thriller genre demands a great deal of precise exposition, Chandler never feeds it to us piecemeal. He breaks up description with dialogue that itself conveys fact. Everything in the books comes to us from Marlowe's point of view and so is in the first person but, as well as coming to us in fragments, what Marlowe reports to us often has to be modified or qualified further downstream. Crucially, not writing from 'significant' personal memory, Chandler/Marlowe knows what to leave out. He tells us Moose Molloy uses golf-balls for buttons on his huge jacket. We aren't told how they are attached. This, of course, is so as not to sacrifice pace and momentum for the specious sake of 'that was how it was' completeness: 'I remember'. But on key occasions Marlowe describes to us what he sees or what he has learnt has happened without telling us how he feels. This is reserved for later, much more telling, explanatory revelation. Thus, to stay with Moose Malloy, we know what this awesomely freakish giant of a man looks like and what he is capable of. It is only as *Farewell, My Lovely* is concluding that we have confirmed for us what – left to our deductions we have rather gathered – that Marlowe has a very genuine affection for this first cousin of Steinbeck's Lenny.

Proust's long wander down memory lane is among the most blatant examples of self regard proving insufficiently fertile soil to nurture a serious novel. The biographical incident in his protagonist's development is not that remarkable enough to warrant writing home about – it might have been if Proust/Marcel had had a proper job, of course – and his reactions are predictable. This would not have been the case if Marcel and the dozens of characters he encounters had been endowed with a three-dimensional quiddity that created a valency with the reader and so an empathy. But we are not engaged. Although Proust came by his characters as Boswell might have done had he tried his hand at writing novels, what he presents for our – what? – entertainment or instruction are no more than types. Proust's self-absorption has allowed him to neglect thoroughly realising them and so, whatever their countless repetition, hesitations or, of course, deviations, we sooner rather than later cease to care. If Proust was intending to lift the veil on a whole new world for us, he need not have bothered. We knew all this anyway and we do not reach the end of his novel any the wiser. If he was intending to deliver a self-portrait he should have been more modest and stayed his hand.

This may all, no doubt, impress as being ten parts digression and rant. But I am seeking to attest to Chandler's finesse in composing *The Long Goodbye*. It is the index of the artistic tact and personal modesty with which he insinuates so much of himself into the narrative in a manner rendered impersonal and objective. It is eloquent of this finesse that (as we probably did the first time around) we can read and enjoy *The Long Goodbye* without needing to know a thing about Chandler's own history or personality. The thriller is self-sufficient. But it is that – a thriller. And as such, it should be acknowledged, distinctly easier for Chandler to exercise his modesty than had he been attempting a 'serious' novel.

In *The Long Goodbye*, as in almost all his stories, Chandler is positing a parallel universe. It is a simpler, more streamlined world than the one we are stuck with. In the thriller world no-one (unless it is a plot point) agonises over a daughter's poor grades at school, the rising price of coffee or global warming. Chandler spends much time in his stories purporting to link the world of private eyes and Mr Bigs. He dilates on fast-food joint rip-offs, traffic snarl ups, schlock tv, for instance. This is in part to ride a few hobby-horses and sound off. It is in part to provide an index for Marlowe's personality. (A guy who denigrates that sort of Chef's Special can't be all bad.) But eventually much stuff and matter of the world we know which appears in the narrative is there to lure us by its familiarity into the parallel universe. Unless, while reading, we feel we are part of Marlowe's world we are not going to become concerned as to what may happen to him. Chandler's Marlowe is artfully (sic) planted in his landscape more firmly than Proust's Marcel is in his.

But Marlowe's world, finally, is not the real world. As we close the book and emerge from the decompression chamber, we know that we have been delivered back from that parallel universe where the whites are whiter and the noirs more noir. And somewhere about this point an ancillary key thought may dawn: in the twentieth century the knight has progressed on from the Paynim villain. These stories in which Marlowe faces down and sometimes thwarts the guys with guns are Morality Plays.

This is another topic we must consider downstream.

Playback

BELATEDLY, DURING PERHAPS MY THIRD OR fourth reading of *The Long Goodbye*, not so much an afterthought but an after-impression came to me. I found myself wondering whether in giving that title to his sixth full-length world Chandler was permitting himself a private indulgence. As a title *The Long Goodbye* is loosely applicable to three or so of the book's major characters and it has, of course, a moody, thrillerish ring. But now I suddenly found myself considering whether the title might not have still further relevance to the author himself. Could this be Chandler bidding farewell to his public as he took his final bow?

Given the different key signature I have argued for, *The Long Goodbye* was never going to fall into the category of those Chandler novels born of that Frankensteinian stitching together of previous plot lines. But it does revisit and re-cycle characters and locations Chandler had previously introduced us to. For no essential reason, for instance, it reacquaints us with Sewell

Endicote, the refined, upright DA of *The Little Sister* now back practising on his own behalf. We again meet Bernie Ohls the tough, efficient, good-guy cop, who has been an intermittent participant in Marlowe stories since the early days of the pulp short stories but never before impacted on the narrative to such effect. We revisit Idle Valley which in *The High Window* had 'the gatehouse at the entrance and the private police force, and the gambling casino on the late, and the fifty dollar joy girls' but which now, post World War II, has become the exclusive fiefdom of Southern California's dubiously privileged drinking set where Marlowe senses himself as blending in as unobtrusively as 'a pearl onion on a banana split'. Set as they are among new versions of Chandler's stock repertory company – Bay City cops, snake-oil medical practitioners, bullet-proof mobsters – these revenant characters and locations put this flimsy thought into my head. I gained a faint sense of a land owner, as it were, making a tour of his estate and affording elements within it he holds affection for a fondly farewell nod of the head as he contemplates his own long goodbye.

Well ... fanciful in the extreme, most probably. The thought has only one arguable saving grace. It would have been better for Chandler's posthumous stock if *The Long Goodbye* had been his final bow.

When in 1958 what was to prove Chandler's last Marlowe thriller was published in England, Maurice Richardson compared it in his review for the *Observer* to a tennis racket whose strings had gone soft. As a simile this is perhaps not as arresting as one of Chandler's own: but, sadly, it is entirely accurate. With *Playback* Chandler's lifetime batting average took a distinct nose dive. Not that there were not extenuating circumstances.

At the end of December 1954, hard on the heels of the publication of *The Long Goodbye*, Cissy Chandler had finally completed her slow wearisome business of dying. Perhaps familiarity with her waning condition over such a long period had bred a kind of contempt in Chandler: if it hadn't happened yet it might never. But when, inevitably, it did, he was devastated.

In the immediate aftermath he recommenced or, as it might have been, continued drinking as heavily as ever. In correspondence to his closest acquaintances that in its very eloquence courts a charge of being self-regarding he said:

> For thirty years, ten months and four days she was the light of my life, my whole ambition. Anything I did was just the fire for her to warm her hands at. That is all there is to say. She was the music heard faintly on the edge of sound.

It is hard to imagine Marlowe or Hammett succumbing to such extravagance. But no more than of the dead, I dare say, we should not speak ill of the bereaved.

Then, in a sense, Chandler was very nearly dead himself. Ten weeks after Cissy's passing, he phoned the La Jolla police to announce that he was about to take his own life. This was not the first time he had made such a call; but they responded anyway. On this occasion they discovered that he had staged what reads as a heavy-handed black parody of the shower-stall killing in *The Lady in the Lake*. Blind drunk he had staggered into his own shower and, by accident or incompetent design, loosed off a shot.

If it had been aimed at his own person, it missed. If he had slipped on the soap, it was but a further stroke of irony. Whatever the intention – genuine attempt at suicide or low comedy cry for help – the end product was Chandler's being clapped up (and this *is* ironic) in a private sanatorium close to the Mexican border. Within a week his prestige and money and friends' influence had seen him self-discharged. (Probably his indignation at this indignity had sobered him and sufficiently restored him to his wits to make this viable.) He was free to go anywhere he chose. Where?

When the world is your oyster 'where' becomes pretty much of a muchness. But equally when we are hurt the impulse to revisit our long-ago golden (as it now seems) past becomes well nigh irreversible. For the next four years, during which we may say with some confidence that he never drew a totally sober breath, Chandler shuttle-cocked backwards and forwards between London and La Jolla. In many ways he found the former the more congenial. The literary intelligentsia of the day had discovered him and had designated him 'classic'. Thus in a sense he gained the *entrée* to that elite Bloomsbury circle which had been denied him forty years earlier. But it was not merely for the pleasure of being honoured that he would book into the Connaught. He had more immediate targets in his sights. Even though when the liquor level was at the given height he would become utterly mawkish about Cissy and claim that on the day of her death his own countdown to the grave had begun in earnest, he was now, on both sides of the Atlantic, courting the company of an increasing number of ladies of a certain age. In almost all instances, sometimes virtually on first acquaintance, he would propose marriage. This is a very sad thing to record because I suspect that on each and every occasion he was thoroughly sincere. Whether he was prompted by memories of former hurt, a deep desire to be mothered, as deep a wish to be paternal, sheer loneliness or frustration with *ad hoc* laundry arrangements is not finally to be discerned, Almost nobody took him seriously. There was, in fact, an instance or two of a gold-digger trying to exploit him or, later, his estate: but in the main, all aware of his states of health and mind, the ladies in question made a laudable, collective effort to cosset his well-being and save him from his worst excesses. He had become in his accelerated old age like Lear at the end of his days, a very foolish, fond old man, or worse, the *alter ego* had engulfed him and he was now a bloated Terry Lennox.

Booze and flirtation can only get you so far through the day. It was against this sorry background that Raymond Thornton Chandler began to write again. There may have been pressure from a publisher ('Ray, it would be great if we could have a new one for the fall list') but the far surer guess is that Chandler began to put doodling pen to paper again because his sad days demanded diversion therapy. *Playback*, I suggest, is most kindly judged if seen as having evolved to meet this need.

It is not, let me say at once, a disaster. There was too much culture and talent still latent in Chandler's attenuated DNA, too much auto-pilot know-how for him to blot his copybook totally. *Playback* is more worthy and entertaining than, say, the latter-day predictably formulaic 'Ian Flemings'. All the same, in *Playback* all of the classic Chandler virtues come distinctly watered down. The book reads like it was yesterday's left-overs re-heated and re-hashed.

Which it was. Once again in the pursuit of gaining traction Chandler, now on the verge of seventy, revisited his past. *Playback* is arguably the most wholesale example of Chandler's auto-cannibalising since he 'sourced' it directly from the screenplay which Universal had commissioned ten years earlier but never put into production. This 'translation' process should not conjure for us an image of Chandler back at Dulwich conning his Virgil with a copy of Dryden's rendering at his side, his index fingers keeping pace to left and right. There is quite a deal of new carpentry in the novel version. Primarily the structure has had to be adapted to accommodate the inclusion of a private eye, Marlowe, into the narrative, who will provide a first-person viewpoint. Since the proximity of an international border has necessary impact on the story but Chandler is now set in his La Jolla ways, Canada becomes Mexico. Various Seattle waterfront capers now go by the board to be replaced by a new sub-plot keyed to a second private investigator from Kansas City, as incompetent as unpleasant. But the main premise of the original screenplay, the MacGuffin that serves as the narrative's armature is identical to both versions.

This MacGuffin is itself based upon a (North Carolina) anomaly, so to call it, in the American legal system. While his exploiting this quirk redounds much to Chandler's credit as a researcher, the loophole it offers appears so tricksy that it is hard to accept that the action of *Playback* takes place in a world that, even bearing in mind we see it through the prism of the thriller genre, seems to have minimum connection with our own. This sense of 'who cares?' alienation is compounded by the plot requiring a coincidental repetition of the story-line's accidental death point of departure that is so implausible it further distances reality and thus leaves our disbelief even more unsuspended. But then so many of the incidental happenings in *Playback* – the punk hoodlum hit man, the dope-taking, mixed-race parking attendant – seem not to arrive organically from the narrative but to be arbitrarily imposed from outside. ('If I introduce a hoodlum here I can work up some tough-guy strong arm stuff from Marlowe that will add pace, fill a few paragraphs and give me an excuse to get the police back in.') Betty Mayfield, the damsel-in-distress heroine of *Playback* struggles to be more than a largely unrealised cipher. According to plotting requirements and her own local initiatives she modulates from little sister to feisty nice girl to femme fatale but she never truly takes on a core personality. In *The Little Sister* Marlowe finally has sex between the covers of a Chandler book. This is with Linda Loring, the acerbically attractive late-thirties something whom it is difficult not to see as a fitting partner for Marlowe. Their encounter seems both appropriate and wholesome. In *Playback*, although she has become his *de facto* client, Marlowe makes a motel play for Betty Mayfield in a manner that seems less than gallant or Marlovian. He is only prevented from having his wicked way by the unlooked-for interruption of a bad guy. Later in the narrative Marlowe does have sex – the nearest to blow-by-blow explicitness Chandler ever gave us – with a Linda Loring stand-in who is utterly incidental to the story-line. Then comes a third encounter. It is again with Betty Mayfield and this time, although we are denied admission Marlowe is unmistakably not. The 'fade out' line of dialogue which takes the pair beyond our ken is possibly the worst one ever to clatter forth from Chandler's typewriter.

'Take me. I'm yours – all of me is yours – take me.'
Ah – *si la veillesse pouvait*.

All these bedroom episodes come across as sops to the increasing permissiveness of the mid-50s publishing scene. The inclusion of the consummated episodes may possibly, of course, have been partly occasioned by Chandler trying to indulge his own wishful thinkingness.

Two episodes in *Playback* are both quite unquestionably indulgences and both distinctly inorganic bolt-ons. The first is embodied in an otherwise utterly functionless minor character who delivers first a paen of praise for Esmeralda, scene of the main action, which I take to be one La Jolla citizen's tribute to his fellow local taxpayers. The character immediately moves on to pay tribute to the honesty and basic decency of a certain specific ethnic group, the Jews. This encomium, coming from nowhere, seems to be Chandler's 'mea culpa' apology for once casting aspersions on all things Jewish with the portrait of the sharply astute coin dealer in *The High Window*. Had a La Jolla neighbour complained to Chandler about this sketch? It is light years away from being Fagin and the coin dealer is presented with far more dispassionate casualness than a dozen of Chandler's various ethnic characters. No apology was called for in the first place and its inclusion in the text of *Playback* is a two-fold editorial blemish.

The second indulgence crudely imposed on the novel is embodied in a character common to both it and the original screenplay, Henry Clarendon IV. Clarendon is a long-term resident of the two hotels in which the respective versions' central murder takes place. Elderly, distinguished and cultivated, a self-confessed 'snob', Clarendon performs a useful function in the novel because, sardonically observing the passing scene in this his native habitat he doesn't miss a trick or nuance. He is thus able to provide Marlowe with some useful information and exposition. Chandler in his last years was embarrassed by his arthritic and mottled hands. He took to wearing white gloves. In the novel he gives this trait to Clarendon and, if we have eyes to see, we come thus to understand that Henry Clarendon IV constitutes something of a self-portrait. We are thus led to believe we should read a certain import into a long speech Chandler accords him.

> I have spent many, many years in lobbies, lounges and bars, on porches, terraces and ornate gardens in hotels all over the world. I have out-lived everyone in my family. I shall go on being useless and inquisitive until the day comes when the stretcher carries me off to some nice airy corner room in a hospital. The starched white dragons will minister to me. The bed will be wound up, wound down. Trays will come with that awful tasteless hospital food. My pulse and temperature will be taken at frequent intervals and invariably when I am dropping off to sleep. I shall lie there and hear the rustle of the starched skirts, the slurring sound of the rubber shoe soles on the aseptic floor, and see the silent horror of the doctor's smile. After a while they will put the oxygen tent over me and draw the screens around the little white bed and I shall, without even knowing it, do the one thing in the world no man ever has to do twice.

Absolutely prescient as it transpired, this passage is Chandler's acknowledgement of his own imminent demise. It demonstrates that even close to being *in extremis* himself, he had not lost his of social comment in Chandler's work, the declaration that personal honour is to be insisted upon; that decency in both private and public life must, if necessary, be fought for in battles where perhaps a brave wit may be the last resource for preserving the awareness of his own integrity left an otherwise defeated man.

But while this may locate Marlowe in an area that goes beyond the purely topographical, it does not go very much further. It lacks the cutting edge and staying power to penetrate that barrier between thriller and the novel proper because its content is not sufficiently profound. The subtext (so to call it) with which Fitzgerald endowed *Gatsby* is.

For who, what, is Gatsby himself? Is he the American Dream shipwrecked in his own shallows? Is he the archetypal adolescent marooned in the banal tragedy of his blind Peter Pan refusal to mature? Is he the idealist unable to understand that in a corrupt and selfish age where Wall Street can fix the World Series there can be no ideals and compromise is a virtue? And does that ideal make him worth the whole damn bunch set together? Is Gatsby's arc the blueprint for the son of another bootlegger, John Fitzgerald Kennedy? Is Daisy's Cressida-like frailty a female universal? With every re-reading fresh thoughts, new shadows of surmises rise up from the subtext Fitzgerald has layered in.

It is the richness of this subtext which gives Fitzgerald the advantage over Chandler paragraph by paragraph and makes his story finally mythic where Chandler's is not. The two men were of the same generation, had the same alcoholic heel and both wrote books with sex and violence at their core. (It is a good old-fashioned MacGuffin, by the way, that makes *The Great Gatsby* work. The car switch focuses the narrative and imbues it with momentum.) But because *Gatsby* does not travel three inches off the ground and is rooted so deeply with so many layers, far many more subtleties work through to its surface. The prose of *The Great Gatsby* can almost be described as poetic, so gracefully apposite is it. It has, you see, so much to be apposite about. Chandler's prose in *The Little Sister* is controlled, varied, cadenced and, of course, always functional. But its rhythms, its tones of voice, and, indeed, the situations and scenes it describes do repeat. It, too, like Chandler's imagination, is imprisoned within the thriller form. Thus it is that just as Lorenz Hart is not Philip Larkin, so Raymond Chandler cannot be Scott Fitzgerald. The two were working in different forms and Fitzgerald's was the one that, because so much more demanding, offered such greater potential. Both writers were attempting to render their material into as gracefully appropriate a finished shape as possible but, given the limit in potential imposed upon him by the genre he had chosen, Chandler could not hope for anything more refined than to confect a 'perfect entertainment'. We may say, not carping, that in this he sometimes succeeded. He leaves us momentarily excited. Fitzgerald, in the instance of *The Great Gatsby* leaves us sadder and more elated and momentarily wiser. 'Yes' we may reply to W.H. Auden, 'Chandler's books may be judged as works of art but they should not be placed on the A list.'

Given, though, that an overwhelming consensus awards Chandler pride of place at the top of the B list the question starts to assert itself that it may represent an enormous lost opportunity – one of literature's great losses – that he never felt sufficiently motivated to attempt an unequivocally 'serious' novel. Surely he might have: surely he was possessed of all the requisite qualities such a work demands. Surely ...

It is not so much very difficult to envisage what form such a hypothetical work would have taken, and in what key it would have been written, as impossible. Would Chandler's assimilation of all things American, the language most of all, have resulted in a leaner, hard-edged improvement upon J.P. Marquand? Would he have delved back to his young Bloomsbury roots and, older now and technically proficient, given us a graceful, more laconically intelligent, stream-of-consciousness novel to place alongside Virginia Woolf's best. An admirer of Maugham's astringency, could Raymond Thornton Chandler have emerged as an American Graham Greene? Hardly. Commenting on Greene's *The Heart of the Matter* he had observed that it fell short of being a good book only through its lack of 'verve, wit, guts, music and magic.' Ah! Guts, magic! Perhaps the stream of consciousness would have been not in the Woolf but the Wolfe manner. Or more wild and whirling still. Perhaps *The Long Goodbye*'s Roger Wade was an *alter ego* he had seriously tried on for size ...

Plainly, trying to posit what manner of 'serious' novelist Chandler might have evolved into is a fool's pursuit. And certainly Chandler thought that in his day and age the game was not worth the candle. The classicist and traditionalist in him – the embryonic scholar who had cut some teeth on Homer and Sophocles and thence gravitated to Shakespeare and Dickens – held an extremely dim view of the accepted literary-cum-intellectual elite of his day. In a letter he wrote to the editor of *Atlantic Monthly* at about the time his personal circumstances would first have allowed him to make this putative gear change, 1947, he in effect asked 'what elite?' Looking about him he was entirely dismissive.

> An eye which is incapable of poetry is incapable of any kind of literature except that cleverness of decadence. The boys can say anything, their scenes are almost tiresomely neat, they have all the facts and all the answers, but they are little men who have forgotten how to pray.

There is, of course, a considerable measure of ring-fencing about this ('If I disparage the whole crew and all their works I don't have to try to beat them at their own game.') but I strongly suspect that the accuracy of Chandler's explicit assessment here is matched by the implicit 'placing' of himself. If he ever did have 'immortal longings' to make an out-and-out attempt to write a novel unequivocally intended to be received as a masterpiece, I believe he was wise to nip the impulse in the bud and pour himself another drink.

Chandler, at last reaching solvency as he reached sixty, would have known by now that he lacked the energy to go out on a highbrow limb. But if the thought had occurred to him in earlier years – as I am sure it must have – he would have had the artistic tact, the duly modest awareness of his own strengths and weaknesses, the sheer common sense not to try putting flesh on the fantasy. His proportionate response was to limit himself in *The Long Goodbye* to pushing the thriller genre envelope to further limits while taking good care not to rupture it and so find himself toppling (as did le Carré, for example, with his gruesomely inept *The Naive and Sentimental Lover*) across a frontier that bordered, not upon the uplands of the adult novelist, but the quicksands of pastiching pretenders. We must be grateful for this self-aware restraint.

Le Carré, to his credit, reoccupying the terrain best suited to his skills, soon regained his storyteller's traction and therewith the earned right to be taken seriously again as he extended the line stretching from *A Scandal in Bohemia* and on through *Green Mantle* on again and down to his own world's grey and compromised version of the Great Game.

Conjuring the presence of the cohabiters of 221B Baker Street into this study provides a convenient link into a topic which, while it is utterly irrelevant to Chandler's output in terms of either literary merit or readership enjoyment, nevertheless solicits attention. As in the case of so many men and women, often 'entertainers' who emerge from obscurity to a prominence lasting beyond the Warholian fifteen minutes, Chandler's reputation eventually became the target of a vindictive backlash. A double-barrelled charge was intermittently levelled against him: he was a misogynist and/or (after all, he had married a woman nearly twenty years his senior) a repressed homosexual.

The irrelevancy of these charges in terms of the work is made clear by the retort 'maybe, so what?' But if we allow them the briefest moment in court that they warrant it has to be conceded that on the misogyny count a *prima facie* circumstantial case may be argued. Witness: in every one of Chandler's first six 'classic' thrillers the core murderer, the setter in train of the whole plot, is a woman. Well, then ... if this of itself be proof positive that Raymond Chandler was a misogynist, then so too were Dashiell Hammett, Alexandre Dumas, Agatha Christie on many an occasion, Gustave Flaubert, Emile Zola and Angela Carter. The precedent set, we would have to expunge from literary culture *The Agamemnon, Medea, The White Devil, King Henry VI (Part III), King Lear, Hedda Gabler, Macbeth, Snow White.* For Starters.

Setting aside the evident truth that across the spread of his books Chandler gave us a significant gallery of nice women – wholesome, witty, loyal, intelligent, sexy in an attractive way, brave – the major plank in rebutting the charge of misogyny is that Chandler was working in an inherited genre in which the *femme fatale* was a staple element and the concept *cherchez la femme* a ubiquitous driver of plot development. Writing for money – to put food on the table and pay the rent – Chandler embraced the form and its conventions. For every duplicitous, malevolent female he described, he gave us a dozen as many male characters. There are a lot of such types in the thriller world.

The most pitifully contemptible argument for Chandler being a woman hater is that Marlowe was too. We know this, you see, because Marlowe is not married. This really is not to see the wood for the trees.

The reason Marlowe has no wife is that to give him one would be to put a severe brake upon pace in the narrative and hugely limit opportunities for suspense. Are we seriously to imagine Marlowe returning home of an evening to face the question, 'Have a good day at the office, honey?' Should we contemplate scenarios wherein as Marlowe lies mugged and drugged in some fake sanatorium his wife is on the line to Missing Persons saying that he should have been home hours ago? It is true that there are crime-fiction double acts, some husband and wife teams. These are Lord Peter and Harriet Vane, there are Nick and Nora Charles (more though on film emulsion than on paper), the Queens *fils et père*, who all follow in the steps of Holmes and Watson. There are innumerable DIs and their assistants in the innumerable different-only-identical police procedure bore-fests that clutter our television screens. But all of these double acts relate to *mystery* stories where the interim dialogue exchanges allow exposition to be laid down and, most importantly of all, the various whodunnit possibilities to be teasingly paraded past the reader or viewer. In the thriller world the protagonist who travels alone travels fastest and more two-fistedly. And, at that deeper level where honour and self-respect have weight, who ever heard of a knight errant that was married? Marlowe's bachelordom is a plotting requirement.

There is a sequence in *The Long Goodbye* which has drawn explicit fire from those pressing charges of misogyny. It is the moment when, waiting to meet a potential client, Marlowe is sitting in the bar of the Ritz-Beverly Hotel where a picture window commands a view of the hotel swimming pool. A blonde whom Marlowe finds distinctly nubile is strutting her starlet-esque stuff around the pool in a white sharkskin swimsuit. Having removed her helmet and shaken 'her bleach job' loose she sits down next to a specimen of beefcake 'with a tan so evenly dark that he couldn't have been anything but the hired man around the pool.' He pats her thigh and at this point Chandler goes for the jugular.

> She opened a mouth like a firebucket and laughed. That terminated my interest in her. I couldn't hear the laugh but the hole in her face when she unzipped her teeth was all I needed.

It has been argued that the brutal finality of this dismissal is proof beyond question that not so deep down Chandler had it in for women. There are two answers to this absurdly shallow charge, the frivolous and the correct.

The frivolous response is that as reportage the incident accurately recalls my own impressions of air-head wannabe bimbos of that Hollywood time and place. Chandler did not need to make the blonde up.

He did, however, choose to. His motive was not unconscious misogyny but the wish to execute a very deliberate piece of craftsmanship. Within minutes of experiencing this 'firebucket' anti-climax, Marlowe is introduced to a second woman. Chandler describes her as if she has just stepped into his pages from a Botticelli canvas. Eileen Wade is all beauty, delicacy, refinement, poise and understated highest style. Chandler has given us the bleached-haired blonde as a coarse-grained contrast that will heighten the impression that he intends Eileen Wade to make. He has an agenda as yet hidden from the reader. There is more – or less – in Eileen Wade than first meets the bedazzled eye. Chandler wishes to delay the moment of our realising this. Introduced as a diversion, the blonde is not Freudian slip give away but literary tactic.

That Chandler on achieving his rather belated measure of prominence should have drawn fire from the homophobic tendency seems to be wretchedly pathetic – in the colloquial sense of the word – on two fronts. It is, to begin with, a thoroughly distasteful attitude to hold that a person's sexual orientation be considered an index of their moral worth. And specifically an author's sexual orientation is irrelevant to the quality of his or her work. What William Shakespeare did or did not like to get up to with the Earl of Southampton has no more bearing on *As You Like It* than whether or not the fourth Earl of Derby wrote it with his left hand.

Sexual orientation, of course – as in *The Well of Loneliness* – may be the driving creative force behind a work: but it is by the text in anonymous isolation that a novel is always to be judged. That Gore Vidal by his own repeated account was more attracted to men than women has no bearing whatsoever on either the local or the architectural quality of his splendidly-achieved historical novel *Burr*. But neither is it relevant to the literary quality of his extraordinarily brave, if melodramatically overwrought, proto-homosexual novel *The City and the Pillar*. We are bound to judge any book on what lies between its covers and not what occurs under those on the author's bed.

Chandler, though, some would have us believe was clearly a (possibly repressed) homosexual. Just consider now! To all intents and purposes he never had a father. As an only son he was looked after by his mother. Later, he looked after her – and quite openly! When, at the advanced age of thirty-six, mark you, he married, it was to a woman nearly twenty years his senior whom, when they were alone he undoubtedly addressed as Jocasta. Oh yes, he did spend long periods of his middle age getting drunker than a skunk and tom-catting around but that was clearly calculated camouflage. The same wish to throw fairy dust in our eyes explains why his stories and novels feature a macho hero and tough guys with guns ... The slur of (alleged) homosexuality once raised, the homophobe, of course, cannot lose. The harder, the crisper, the more masculine the textual evidence before his eyes, the more the repressed author is over-compensating. Only the naivest of critics would believe that Chandler wrote tough, action-packed private-eye thrillers simply because that was where the money was and because it was something that, being poor, he had taken the trouble to learn how to do well.

Apart from Chandler's own snide side-swipes at two-dimensional, stereotypical homosexuals in the first novel-thriller *The Big Sleep* (jibes largely linked to the pornographic book dealer, Geiger) there is one other locus in his work that the subject of (male) sexual deviancy is actively addressed. Since I have insisted that the work, is everything, I must, I suppose, indulge this red herring a moment longer. The book in question is *The Long Goodbye*.

In this late novel-thriller the most malign, though deranged, figure is a woman; but the foreground of the narrative is, as we have seen, dominated by the three male characters, Marlowe, Terry Lennox and Roger Wade. The paths of the latter two, although they are old acquaintances, do not cross within the text. Consecutively, however, Marlowe does the most terrible things with both of them. He sits and talks to them over drinks. He uses his car to help them out of jams. He does what little he can to help them lay off the sauce. It becomes clear that although he has some major reservations in both instances, he rather admires and respects certain qualities the two men possess and so is inclined to like them both. Well! The idea! That grown men should entertain the possibility of friendship! But look! In *The Long Goodbye* Roger Wade actually has the effrontery to give voice concerning that type of love that should not speak its name. Deeply drunk he declares to Marlowe:

'I had a male secretary once. Used to dictate to him. Let him go. He bothered me sitting there waiting for me to create. Mistake. Ought to have kept him. Word would have got around I was a homo. The clever boys that write reviews because they can't write anything else would have caught on and started giving me the build up. Have to take care of their own, you know. They are all queers, every damn one of them. The queer is the artistic arbiter of our age, chum. The pervert is the top guy now. '
'That so? Always been around, hasn't he?'

There is no plot reason for making Wade mention this long ago and far away amanuensis. Just possibly there is a subtextual one. Wade is half off his face as he speaks from the alcohol in his system and even more so from the noxious cocktail of self-disgust and unspeakable knowledge that possess him. He has come to loathe himself because he now discerns that self to be a sham: the work he is so much applauded for is without merit. The knowledge he must live with – that he *does* know, Chandler quietly makes explicit in the book's final exchange – is that his wife has committed a horrendous crime. Hit from within and without by this terrible combination Wade has found his world reeling. He has no place to stand. Now it is just possible to conceive that acknowledging the existence of a homosexual world at this point, may be understood as Chandler suggesting yet another guilt-ridden reason for Wade to have 'fallen out of love with myself'. But I doubt this. I believe this brief section is an instance of an author indulging himself.

Chandler, it seems to me, has introduced us to the sacked secretary so as to convert Roger Wade into a dummy through whom he can ventriloquize an in-passing rant against the homosexual New York literary Mafia (real or imagined) whom he – Chandler – sees denigrating his own work. Our ears should tell us this is so. Chandler prefaces Wade's diatribe by having Marlowe tell us 'his voice suddenly seemed much more clear' but what the voice most seems like is that Wade is reading from one of Chandler's own acerbic letters to a fellow writer. The real beef here is as much against the critical as the homosexual coterie: but, put into the mouth of a character in a work of fiction, demotically anti-gay it is. Chandler's homophobic foes will at once counter that this is more camouflage: a case of him protesting too much. I do not think so. I do not think any closet-repressed homosexual writing in the fifties would have used the word pervert, even as a diversionary tactic, about a persuasion towards which he had (or suspected he might have) sympathy.

What is eloquent in this passage, I would argue, is Marlowe's reply to Wade's complaint.

'That so? Always been around, hasn't he?'

For me this conversational shrug of the shoulders, civilised, humane, sensible in its 'so what?' acceptance should be taken to pinpoint Chandler's own latter-day attitude towards the natural phenomenon, the everyday reality, of homosexuality. We can see in it too, I would like to think, just the hint of an apology for his earlier cheap *Big Sleep* pops at gay stereotypes. That was what the pulp market of those days not only could bear but rather expected. Fifteen years on this attitude may not have seemed so couth. A sliver of olive branch might perhaps be extended.

After fifteen years Chandler at last allows Marlowe to go to bed with a woman within the traffic of one of his cases. In part, I think, this is because the notional Hays Act that had lingered about the middle-class world of popular fiction had by now all but evaporated. The posture of 'realism' that the thriller required demanded by now that Marlowe do a little more than leer at the occasional blonde, refer back to a past fling or reject the naked overtures of a tacky nymphomaniac. It had to be more positively demonstrated that the knight in tarnished armour still had red blood in his veins. Thus in *The Long Goodbye* Marlowe sleeps with Linda Loring. But in brokering this union Chandler is doing more than pander to an increasingly permissive climate of acceptance. He takes care to ensure that Marlowe's core integrity is not compromised. Linda Loring is a poised and informed woman well able to make discriminating and adult choices for herself. That she chooses Marlowe reflects well on him. Further, Marlowe comes upon her at a time when she is in the process of divorcing her first husband – so odiously complacent and self-important a creep that we wonder (it is a blemish) how she could have married him in the first place. Marlowe helps rescue the damsel thus distressed from this pip-squeak ogre. Not only that, she is no casual fling. He cares. When she in effect proposes to him – and money is no problem; she is loaded – it is a major source of grief to him that there is unfinished business to take care of that no knight worthy of the name could ride away from.

For the homophobic critic the encounter with Linda Loring is just so much more over-compensation on the part of the repressed author. She is, that is to say, a beard. On a grown-up level though, it does have to be conceded that in creating her Chandler also made a rod for his own back.

In due course, Cissy dead and his powers now failing, Chandler brought Linda Loring back to provide an essentially extraneous fillip to the end of the flaccid *Playback*, a book in which Marlowe's overt sex life is dilated upon in a distinctly less chivalrous manner. Here, in order to draw some sort of line under petered-out proceedings, she phones in an eleventh-and-a-half-hour appearance. But in the doodle which Chandler was therapeutically occupying himself with as, now that very fond and foolish old man, he tottered glass in hand towards those starched white dragons, Linda Loring is given plumb centre pride of place. She is now Mrs Philip Marlowe and this relationship is the over-riding concern of such narrative as the fragment contains. It abundantly answers the original question – and to be fair to Chandler this is precisely what he wanted to demonstrate – why Marlowe could never have had, and never should have had, a wife.

Marlowe's joust with Linda Loring leaves him with lance unshivered and still mounted upon his charger. And indeed as *The Long Goodbye* concludes, we find him very much on his high horse. When Terry Lennox, his features now altered by plastic surgery to give him an appearance matching his new Mexican identity, pays that visit to Marlowe's office he finds that his erstwhile rescuer, the dog-eared knight whose respect he now so much needs, will not compromise his private-eye's vows. Withholding his pity, Marlowe compels Lennox to walk away without the consolation of friendship and any possibility of the redemption it might lead to.

The completeness of this rejection, let it be pointed out, offers yet another custard pie in the face for the homophobic critic. The two casual acquaintances have not become bosom buddies and there will now be nothing for it but to try to detect homoerotic undertones the next time Marlowe is set upon by the hoods or the law. (A process of thought which may, in turn, bring to mind the pot/kettle axis.)

This, of course, is a pleasing conclusion. But on a serious level, I personally find that the banishing of Lennox to oblivion jars.

It seems to me that in behaving as he does Marlowe is preserving his honour at the expense of his humanity. There is a holier-than-thou intransigence about his remaining true to his principles that smacks not of the lapsed Quaker mind-set Chandler was born into but of some ultra-(self)righteous Puritan sect. Marlowe's Hammett-like hard-mindedness allows Chandler to draw a final line under his story, of course, but I believe, a nobler because more redemptive, conclusion would have been achieved if he had turned back to the last leaf of his short story 'Smart-Aleck Kill'. There after an investigation has ended in a depressingly ragged end, private eye and honest cop face each other over a bottle. 'What'll we drink to?' the cop asks. 'Let's just drink,' the eye replies.

Marlowe as a latter-day knight is one of the two cliché conceptions that recur time and again in discussion of Chandler's books. The other is the quasi-image, begotten by Chandler himself, of the mean streets down which his protagonist hero must proceed. Thereby hangs a misapprehension which it would be remiss not to consider.

It is a third commonplace to associate Raymond Chandler with the genre of *noir* fiction. Blurbs on paperback editions, articles in magazines regularly refer to him as the 'master' or the 'doyen' of *noir* crime fiction. The truth, though, is that he is not: not because he has superiors in what he wrote but because, born of the pulp tradition and hard boiled though his stories may be, they are not *noir*.

We speak of *noir* because – *quelle surprise* – we derive the term from the French and their coining it just after the Second World War. At that time, the French were experiencing a goodly number of *mauvaises quart d'heures* joined back to back. They were in the mood for a luxurious gloom-and-doom wallow in those lower depths that pessimism reaches down to. A distinct species of fiction, more pulp than not, became established whose single most defining feature was that it unrelievedly purveyed protagonists who were, or were to become, losers. Usually from the start these are lost souls doomed by hostile circumstance and more so by the flaws in their own character and intelligence. Less than moral, often on the wrong side of the law (as is often their entire *milieu*) they lay plans to realise impossible dreams and struggle to escape their poverty or impress the woman they obsess over or avoid detection or protect a loved one still more unfortunate than themselves. But it all ends in tears. In defeat and death.

This is not Marlowe's world. Yes, he does indeed go down streets that are mean and the world he encounters there is often hard and cynical and vicious and sordid. But the salient underlying fact is that Marlowe is seen to emerge at the street's further end. He may not emerge unscathed. He emerges as a rule a little sadder and scarcely wiser. But he has survived.

And there is more. His travails will have earned him a measure of victory. Such victories may be Pyrrhic in the main but a quantum of solace will have been arrived at: a crime will have been solved, a crimp, for however brief a period, put into the plans of a crook or a crooked official. More crucial still, hard and persistent though Marlowe will show himself to be, he will not emerge from the mean streets himself made mean. The viciousness of what he encounters does not leech into his soul. He remains untarnished and so, as his story ends, left with a modicum of hope. On a good day perhaps we could be like this too.

On the other hand, on a bad day it is only too easy to identify with the hopelessness and countless human shortcomings of the *noir* protagonists. The genre was no sooner established than immensely popular. Americans and English almost know it best from its shift sideways into the cinema. Films such as *Le Doulos* and *Ascenseur pour l'échafaud* where moody cinematography gave heightened meaning to the generic term and so accelerated the influence of *noir* across frontiers.

Certainly in America and contemporaneously with Chandler an elite cadre of writers was giving us a number of admirable instances of pure *noir* novels which have endured. These writers shared pulp roots with Chandler but, while his calendar contemporaries, they travelled parallel avenues.

Among the best of them are David Goodis (*The Burglar*), Geoffrey Homes (*Build My Gallows High*) and the prolific Cornell Woolrich. All three men, it may be fairly said, led lives more despairingly dysfunctional than Chandler and the nihilism that comes to pervade their pages often reads as witheringly authentic.

There is another strand that can be plaited into the definition of *noir*: that presentation of a world which the author posits as being essentially amoral and so at the mercy of a protagonist without mercy. This opens the door on subject matter that we would call black without any assistance from the French – sadism, masochism, (sexual) violence of the perverse kind, psychopathic deviance. For those with a taste for *noir* without the gloves on (but maybe with the cuffs) Jim Thompson's very variable output includes a handful of powerhouse performances in sustained, black-humoured cynicism.

Arguably the most despairing American *noir* writer of all is David Goodis. And where his focus is chiefly on the lost lives of his rat-trapped characters rather than the mechanics of cops-and-robbers capers, he perhaps comes nearest to penetrating the barrier which separates the thriller from the 'straight' novel. In *The Moon in the Gutter*, for instance, he comes so very close to touching distance with the Nelson Algren of *Never Come Morning* that we might start to talk of the Philadelphia School of Realism. That Goodis does not quite give us a pure novel is because, like Chandler, he is obliged to employ melodrama to progress narrative. But we should not let our judgement be browbeaten by any elitist theory of categories. Whatever the respective veins in which they chose to write, Goodis on a good day is a better novelist than Updike on any.

To finish a reading of *The Moon in the Gutter* is to feel chastened: to feel we have just read a cautionary tale. To finish a Chandler is to feel cheered. We have just read a morality play where virtue, though perhaps not prodigally rewarded, has come out on top. There is life in it, point to it, yet. En reading route we have been exhilarated by frequent injections of wit and there has been something subtly, sub-consciously even, life-affirming about the finesse with which the prose has been assembled and polished in the cause of accomplishing Chandler's ends as storyteller and commentator.

Chandler, in fine, delivers a tonic effect. He achieves this most obviously, perhaps, by that ability of his to give us narrative travelling those crucial few inches off the ground – a quality that Goodis cannot concern himself with when he is deploying characters whose defining characteristic is that they are at the bottom of the pile. Chandler achieves his narrative's elevation not by excluding the mean, the sordid, the venal, the fake, the greedy, the vicious, the murderous. Far from it. What he excludes is the boring. Much of Chandler's own life was boring (it comes included with poverty) but, other than on Page One in his lonely office, Marlowe never was nor is bored or boring. When we put down a just re-read Chandler we feel that our own lives may be that much less of a bore. And perhaps for a while they are.

This is not so negligible a literary achievement.

Bibliography

Chandler Editions

Paperback copies of Chandler's fiction have been a constant on the shelves of high-street/shopping mall booksellers for a good half century. *Penguin* and *Vintage* are the two most high-profile imprints. Penguin have constantly 'refreshed the brand' by 'updating' the covers. Annoyingly, the short stories are not all to be found in a single paperback volume.

First editions, of course, are like gold dust. For those insisting upon a hardback edition for their personal libraries, the *Library of America*'s 1995 two-volume edition of essentially the complete works will seem an attractive acquisition.

It speaks eloquent volumes that second/tenth-hand copies of Chandler books are seldom to be found on the shelves of charity shops.

Chandler's Letters

Due to his need to be on call for his chronically ill wife for so long, Chandler became a prolific letter writer. Those he received and those he wrote to Cissy he took care to burn. Scores of those he despatched remain extant. Since he was not averse to wearing his dislikes and enmities on his epistolary sleeve a high proportion of these are, apparently, too scurrilous, libellous or obscene to bear the light of public day. But many more were preserved by their very various recipients and these have since been collated and published in three distinct selections.

The earliest is *Raymond Chandler Speaking* (Hamish

Hamilton, 1962/Four Square, 1966) edited by Dorothy Gardiner and Kathrine Sorley Walker. Sensibly these co-editors divided the letters into eight categories – *Chandler on Chandler*, *Chandler on the Craft of Writing*, etc. – progressing each one in turn chronologically. A distinct sense of the man and his opinions begins to emerge. But a word of warning: we are all hypocrites when we write letters. We cut the cloth of our correspondence to suit our destination coteries. Philip Larkin, for instance, is not the same man when writing to Barbara Pym as he was to Vernon Scannell. This phenomenon of emphasis shift is clearly there in Chandler and needs to be allowed for.

A later edition of the letters is *The Selected Letters of Raymond Chandler* (Jonathan Cape, 1982). The compiler was Frank MacShane who was co-editor with Tom Hiney of a third option for those seeking to lay hands on a convenient collation, *The Raymond Papers: Selected Letters and Non-Fiction 1909-1959* (Hamish Hamilton, 2000).

MacShane had previously edited some of Chandler's surviving note books, *Notebooks* (Ecco Press (USA) 1976/ Weidenfeld and Nicholson, 1977).

Biographies

MacShane and Hiney made something of a fiefdom and growth market from Chandler's literary relicts. Both wrote biographies. These are: *The Life of Raymond Chandler*, Frank MacShane (Jonathan Cape, 1976). *Raymond Chandler: A Biography*, Tom Hiney (Atlantic Monthly Press, 1977/Chatto and Windus, 1977/ Vintage 1998).

Both lives are very serviceable. Both are better (as they should be) in charting Chandler's course through life than critically 'placing' that life's work or Chandler among contemporary writers.

Hiney's book contains occasional clunkers (Howard Hughes most decidedly did not direct the film of *The Big Sleep*; the houseboy in *The Long Goodbye* is not Guatemalan) but, eschewing that kind of academic inclusiveness that details the menu each time Dickens breakfasts with Longfellow, he gives a very pleasing clarity to the outline of Chandler's life and career.

A third biography, *A Mysterious Something in the Light*, Tom Williams (Aurum, 2012) is surplus to all requirements. It may list a few hiterto unremarked, temporary addresses in the Chandlers' nomadic LA existence but, its critical assessments, shallow and occasionally based on inaccuracies, is couched in prose slovenly enough to make its subject's skelton kick a hole in its coffin.

Those with coffee tables possessed of a high IQ and a liking for nostalgia will find interest in *Raymond Chandler's Los Angeles*, Elizabeth Ward and Alain Silver (Overlook Press, New York, 1957) an 'attempt to illustrate photographically Chandler's literary odyssey through Los Angeles'. The book juxtaposes moody black and white (Kodalith?) cityscape stills with apposite quotations from the books. The format serves to underline how good Chandler's prose was.

There are, of course, today innumerable articles and entries on the internet spinning their way off from Chandler's legacy. Do feel free to add to the confusion.

INDEX

A Foreign Affair 133
A Scandal in Bohemia 179
A Tales of Two Cities 66
Across the Pacific 114
Action Detective (magazine) 27
Alfred A. Knopf (person and publishing house) 18, 47, 48, 49, 50, 68, 108, 141
Algren, Nelson
  Never Come Morning 192
All Quiet on the Western Front 33
All Through the Night 114
Atlantic Monthly (magazine) 177
Ascenseur pour l'échafaud 191
Auden, W.H. 176
Austen, Jane 59

Barris, Alex 35
Bates, H.E. 110
Becall, Lauren 48
Belloc, Hilaire 39
Bendix, William 136, 138
Best Years of Our Lives 136
Black Mask (magazine) 17, 18, 27, 28, 47, 50, 68, 70
Bloomsbury 177
Bloomsbury circle 165
Body and Soul 134
Bogart, Humphrey 48, 132
Boswell, James 160
Brackett, Charles (Charlie) 94, 126
Bromfield, Louis 27

Bryon, Lord George
  Childe Harold 125

Cain, James M. 19, 125, 126, 130, 132
  Double Indemnity 126
  Mildred Pierce 126
  The Postman Always Rings Twice 126
Carter, Angela 179
Casablanca 99
Chandler, Cissy (wife) 17, 20, 21, 23, 47, 74, 110, 123, 138, 143, 144, 153, 164, 165, 171, 187, 195
Chandler, Florence Thornton (mother) 13, 16, 17
Chandler, Maurice (father) 13
Chandler, Raymond
  'Bay City Blues' 109, 119
  'Blackmailers Don't Shoot' 18, 28, 30, 31, 35, 36, 41, 61
  Farewell, My Lovely 18, 19, 77, 78, 81, 82, 83, 84, 85, 87, 88, 90, 91, 92, 98, 104, 105, 125, 159
  'Finger Man' 43, 70
  'I'll Be Waiting' 43, 45
  'Killer in the Rain' 49, 50, 51, 52, 61
  Law is Where You Buy It 111
  'Mandarin's Jade' 78, 92
  'No Crime in the Mountains' 109, 113, 114
  'Pearls are a Nuisance' 37, 38

'Pick-up on Noon Street' 40
Playback 20, 22, 140, 141, 163, 166, 167, 168, 169, 171, 188
'Poodle Springs' 23
'Smart-Aleck Kill' 41, 189
The Big Sleep 18, 19, 33, 43, 48, 49, 51, 52, 56, 57, 58, 59, 61, 65, 66, 67, 77, 78, 81, 84, 118, 125, 173, 184, 197
The Blue Dahlia 19, 136, 138, 140, 154
'The Curtain' 49, 50, 51, 52, 55, 56, 61, 143
'The Gentle Art of Murder' 104
The High Window 18, 19, 77, 94, 97, 98, 99, 100, 101, 103, 104, 105, 106, 107, 108, 109, 115, 121, 125, 163, 169
'The Lady in the Lake' (short story) 109
The Lady in the Lake 18, 109, 110, 111, 112, 113, 114, 115, 117, 119, 120, 123, 164
The Little Sister 20, 77, 163, 168, 174, 176
The Long Goodbye 21, 142, 143, 144, 145, 147, 148, 150, 154, 155, 156, 157, 160, 162, 163, 164, 177, 178, 181, 184, 187, 188, 197
The Second Murderer 92
'Try The Girl' 78
Christie, Agatha 179
Cohen, Leonard 172
Crossfire 134, 136

Dabney Oil Syndicate 16, 26
Dickens, Charles 31, 59, 177, 197

DiMaggio, Joe 105
Dime Detective Monthly (magazine) 27
Dos Passos, John 54
Double Indemnity 19, 48, 94, 130, 132, 133, 134, 136, 139
    Academy Award 132, 134
Dryden, John 167
Dulwich College 13, 14, 15, 25, 27, 31, 32, 33, 34, 39, 51, 60, 74, 75, 93, 140, 167
    Marlowe House 74
Dumas, Alexandre 179
Dylan, Bob 172

Ellroy, James
    LA Confidential 72

Faulkner, William 31
Fitzgerald, F. Scott 95, 145, 173, 174, 175, 176
Flaubert, Gustave 98, 179
Force of Evil 134
Ford, Madox Ford 49
Freud, Sigmund 101

Gardner, Erle Stanley 28, 32, 37, 98
Garner, James 132
Gilkes, A.H. 13, 33
Goodis, David 191, 192, 193
Gould, Elliott 132
Grable, Betty 126, 136
Green Mantle 179
Greene, Graham 84, 177
    The Heart of the Matter 177

Hamish Hamilton 18, 34, 134, 140, 196
Hammett, Dashiell 17, 18, 27, 29, 30, 32, 46, 67, 71, 72, 73, 74, 112, 156, 164, 179, 189
   The Glass Key 46
   The Golden Horseshoe 46
   The Maltese Falcon 67
Handel, G.F. 50
Hart, Lorenz 172, 176
Hawks, Howard 19, 48, 50, 65, 133
Hays Act 187
Hays Office 125, 130, 126
Haymes, Dick 126
Hayworth, Rita 105
Hedda Gabler 180
Hemingway, Ernest 54
Hergesheimer, Joseph 27
Herrick, Robert 50
Highsmith, Patricia
   Strangers on a Train 20, 139
Hiney, Tom 74, 115, 116, 196, 197
Hirst, Damien 123
Hitchcock, Alfred 20, 139, 140
Hickox, Sid 48
Hokusai 50
Holden, William 132
Homer 27, 64, 177
Homes, Geoffrey 191
Housman, John 135
Hudson, W.H. 110

In a Lonely Place 134

James, Henry 58, 59

Keaton, Buster 133
Kennedy, John Fitzgerald 175
King Henry VI (Part III) 180
King Lear 180
Kings Row 101
Knopf, Blanche 103

Ladd, Alan 19, 135, 136, 137
Larkin, Philip 151, 176, 196
le Carré, John 178, 179
Le Doulos 191
Leave Her to Heaven 101

MacMurray, Fred 131, 132
   The Apartment 131
   The Caine Mutiny 131
Marlowe, Christopher (also referred to as Kit Marlowe) 75
Marquand, J.P. 177
Marshall, George 137
Maugham, Somerset 92, 177
Medea 180
Mermaid Tavern 31
Michaelangelo 96
Mildred Pierce 126, 133
Mitchum, Robert 132
Monet, Claude 50
Monroe, Marilyn 129
Montgomery, Robert 132
Mosley, Walter 40

Observer 163
Out of the Past 134

Paramount 19, 20, 106, 124, 126,

131, 132, 134, 135, 138, 139
Pascal, Cissy 16, 17
Paxton, Joseph
   Crystal Palace 57
Perelman, S.J. 35
Farewell, My Lovely Appetiser 35
Pirandello, Luigi 156
Powell, Dick 132
Powell, Anthony 49
Powell, Dawn 54
Proust, Marcel 69, 159, 160, 161

Raft, George 131
Remarque, Erich Maria 138
Rembrandt 50, 105, 106
Rhys, Jean 49
Richardson, Maurice 163
RKO 19
Royal Air Corps 15

Saboteur 114
Sayers, Dorothy L. 104
Shakespeare, William 27, 31, 93, 177, 182
Richard III 31, 92
Sidney, Sir Philip 75
Simenon, Georges 98
Sistrom, Joe 124, 126, 127, 129
Snow White 180
Some Like it Hot 133
Sophocles 177
Stanwyck, Barbara 131
Strangers on a Train 20, 139, 140
Sturges, Preston 133

Sunset Boulevard 133

Tarkington, Booth 27
Teapot Dome Scandal 58
The Agamemnon 180
The Catcher in the Rye 173
The Great Gatsby 173, 175, 176
The Lost Weekend 135
The Moon in the Gutter 192
The Odyssey 157
The Postman Always Rings Twice 126, 133
The Saturday Evening Post 43
The Sound of Fury 134
The Well of Loneliness 183
The White Devil 180
The Whitsun Weddings 172
Thompson, Jim 192
Thornton, Ernest 13
Trevor, William 49

Undercover 101
Universal (Studios) 20, 140, 167
Updike, John 192

Vidal, Gore
   The City and the Pillar 183
Virgil 167
von Stroheim, Erich 129

Warner Brothers 19, 20, 126
Welles, Orson 133, 135
   Mercury Theatre 135
Westminster Gazette 15
Wilder, Billy 19, 94, 106, 126, 127,

128, 129, 131, 132, 133, 134, 139, 140
Willis, Bruce 122
Wodehouse, P.G. 39
Wolfe, Tom 177
Woolf, Virginia 177
Woolrich, Cornell 191
World War I 25, 75, 138, 152
World War II 48, 112, 113, 114, 149, 151, 163, 190

Zola, Émile 179